Choral Connections

LEVEL 1
TREBLE VOICES

GLENCOE

McGraw-Hill

New York, New York
Columbus, Ohio
Mission Hills, California
Peoria, Illinois

Cover Photos: Paul Chen/Masterfile and Eureka Collection/SuperStock, Inc.

Glencoe/McGraw-Hill

A Division of The **McGraw·Hill** *Companies*

Send all inquiries to:
Glencoe/McGraw Hill
15319 Chatsworth Street
Mission Hills, California 91345

ISBN 0-02-655529-8 (Student's Edition)
ISBN 0-02-655543-3 (Teacher's Wraparound Edition)

Printed in the United States of America.

1 2 3 4 5 6 7 8 9   MAL   02 01 00 99 98 97 96

Meet the Authors

Senior Author
Mollie G. Tower—As Coordinator of Choral and General Music of the Austin Independent School District, Mollie Tower was recently nominated as "Administrator of the Year." She is very active in international, national, regional, and state music educators' organizations. Ms. Tower was contributing author, consultant, and reviewer for the elementary programs *Share the Music* and *Music and You*. Senior author of *Música para todos, Primary and Intermediate Dual Language Handbooks for Music Teachers*, she has also written and consulted for many other publications. A longtime advocate of music education, Mollie is a popular clinician who conducts workshops across the country.

Marc Erck
Choir Director
Hill Country Middle School
Austin, Texas

Ruth Phillips
Choir Director
Ruth Phillips has taught choral music in junior high and middle school for 17 years in both the Dallas/Fort Worth area and in San Marcos, Texas. She is currently in her eighth year at Goodnight Junior High. Ms. Phillips received a Bachelor of Science degree in All Level Music Education from McMurry University in Abilene, Texas.

Linda S. Wyatt
Choir Director
With 27 years of choir directing experience, Linda S. Wyatt is presently Director of Choirs at Murchison Middle School in Austin, Texas. After receiving her Bachelor of Music Education degree from Southwest Texas State University, she taught at John Marshall High School and Sul Ross Middle School in San Antonio.

Consulting Author

Dr. Susan Snyder has taught all levels of vocal music over the last 25 years. She holds a B.S. in music education from the University of Connecticut and an M.A. from Montclair State College. She holds a PhD. in curriculum and instruction from the University of Connecticut and advanced professional certificates from Memphis State University and the University of Minnesota. Teaching at Hunter College and City University of New York, Dr. Snyder was coordinating author of the elementary music program, *Share the Music*, and a consultant on *Music and You*. She has published many articles on music education and integrated curriculum and is an active clinician and master teacher.

Consultants

Choral Music
Stephan P. Barnicle
Choir Director
Simsbury High School
Simsbury, Connecticut

Vocal Development, Music Literacy
Katherine Saltzer Hickey, D.M.A.
University of California at Los Angeles
Los Angeles, California
Choir Director
Pacific Chorale Children's Choruses
Irvine, California

Music History
Dr. Kermit Peters
University of Nebraska at Omaha
College of Fine Arts
Department of Music
Omaha, Nebraska

Contributors/Teacher Reviewers

Dr. Anton Armstrong
Music Director and Conductor, St. Olaf Choir
St. Olaf College
Northfield, Minnesota

Jeanne Julseth-Heinrich
Choir Director
James Madison Middle School
Appleton, Wisconsin

Caroline Lyon
Ethnomusicologist
University of Texas at Austin
Austin, Texas

Caroline Minear
Supervisor
Orange County School District
Orlando, Florida

Judy Roberts
Choir Director
Central Junior High School
Moore, Oklahoma

Dr. A. Byron Smith
Choir Director
Lincoln High School
Tallahassee, Florida

Table of Contents

Preparatory Material

Notes and Note Values

1 Whole Note

equals

2 Half Notes

equal

4 Quarter Notes

equal

8 Eighth Notes

equal

16 Sixteenth Notes

Rests and Rest Values

1 Whole Rest

equals

2 Half Rests

equal

4 Quarter Rests

equal

8 Eighth Rests

equal

16 Sixteenth Rests

Rhythm Challenge in 4/4 Time

Directions: Accurately count and/or perform the following rhythms without stopping!

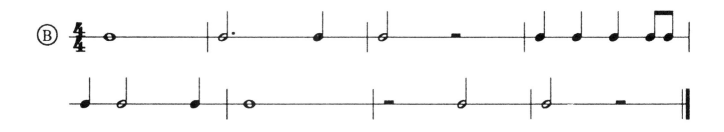

Rhythm Challenge in 6/8 Time

Directions: Accurately count and/or perform the following rhythms without stopping!

Breathing Mechanics

Singing well requires good breath control. Support for singing comes from correct use of the breathing mechanism. Deep, controlled breathing is needed to sustain long phrases in one breath. Also, correct breathing will support higher, more difficult passages.

Posture
Posture is very important in breath support.
- Keep your body relaxed, but your backbone straight.
- To stretch your back: Bend over and slowly roll your back upward until you are standing straight again. Do this several times.
- Hold your rib cage high, but keep your shoulders low and relaxed.
- Facing front, keep your head level. Imagine you are suspended by a string attached to the very top of your head.
- When you stand, keep your knees relaxed and do not "lock" them by pushing them all the way back. Keep your feet slightly apart.
- When you sit, keep both feet flat on the floor and sit forward in your chair.

Inhaling
- Expand the lungs out and down, pushing the diaphragm muscle down.
- Inhale silently without gasping or making any other noise.
- Imagine taking a cool sip of air through a straw.
- Expand your entire waistline, keeping the shoulders low and relaxed.

Breath Control
To help you develop breath control do the following:
- Hold one finger about six inches from your mouth imagining that your finger is a birthday candle. Now blow out a steady stream of air to blow out the flame of the candle.

Summary

STANDING
Feet slightly apart
Knees relaxed
Backbone straight
Rib cage high
Shoulders low
Head level

SITTING
Feet on the floor
Sit on edge of chair
Backbone straight
Rib cage high
Shoulders low
Head level

Solfège and Hand Signs

Solfège is a system designed to match notes on the staff with specific interval relationships. Hand signs provide additional reinforcement of the pitch relationships.

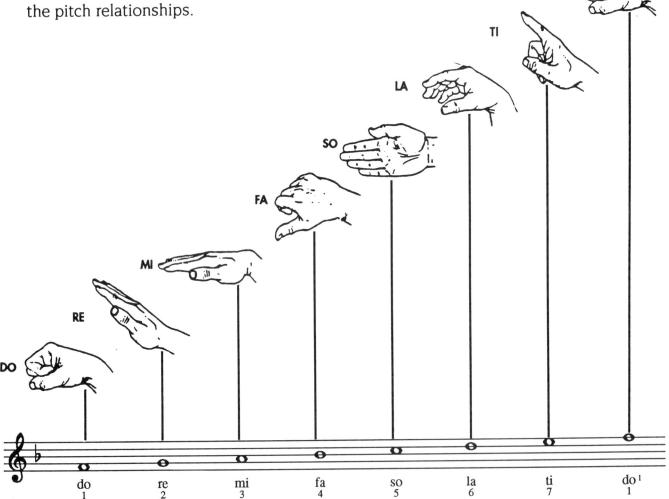

Frequently Found Intervals

An interval is the distance between two notes.

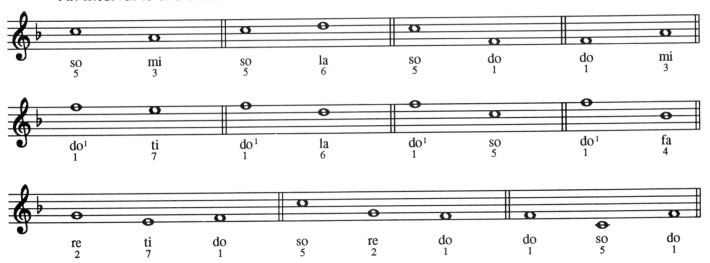

Pitch Challenge

Directions: Accurately sing each measure on solfège using hand signs and without stopping! During the measure of rest, look ahead to the next challenge.

Lessons

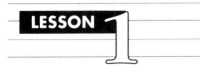

This Train Goes Marching In

ARRANGER: *Sandy Feldstein*

CHORAL MUSIC TERMS

posture

sight-singing

singing parts
  independently

solfège

VOICING

Two part

PERFORMANCE STYLE

Moderately
Accompanied by piano

FOCUS

- Identify and demonstrate the characteristics of correct singing posture.
- Read and sing solfège in E♭ major.
- Perform one of two parts independently.

Warming Up

 Rhythm Drill

Clap this drill in two parts. Notice the imitation.

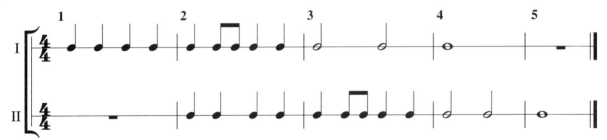

 Vocal Warm-Up 1

Sing this tonic triad exercise using a pulsed (laughing) breath. Repeat the exercise, moving up by half steps.

 Vocal Warm-Up 2

Sing this exercise using solfège and hand signs or numbers, then repeat it singing smoothly on the syllable *loo.* Repeat the exercise, moving up by half steps.

Sight-Singing

Sight-sing these exercises using solfège and hand signs or numbers. Sing each in unison first, then sing in two parts. Notice the imitation.

 Singing: "This Train Goes Marching In"

A rag doll is made without any stiff parts, so that it feels very limp and floppy. Pretend you are a rag doll. Hang limp from your waist up. Slowly roll up each vertebrae of your backbone to the base of your skull. You are now in correct singing position.

Now turn to the music for "This Train Goes Marching In" on page 4.

HOW DID YOU DO?

? ?

"This Train Goes Marching In" started you on a journey of vocal development and part singing. Think about your preparation and performance of "This Train Goes Marching In."

1. What did you do well?

2. What did you have trouble with?

3. Identify and demonstrate characteristics of correct singing posture.

4. Can you read with solfège and hand signals? Choose a part you can sing to demonstrate.

5. Choose a part of "This Train Goes Marching In" to sing with a few classmates in two parts.

6. What can you do to improve?

This Train Goes Marching In

Arranged by
Sandy Feldstein

Two-part with Piano

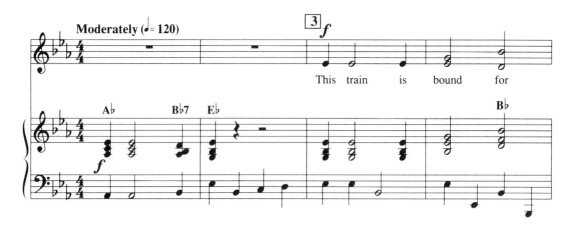

this train. — This train is bound for glo-ry, if you ride it you must be ho-ly.

B♭7 **E♭** **A♭**

This train is bound for glo-ry, this train. —

E♭ **C7**

17 *f*

This train don't take your mon-ey, this train. —

F

This train don't take your mon-ey, this train. —

C7

LESSON 2

Lift Up Your Voice, Alleluia

CHORAL MUSIC TERMS
diction
consonants
independent part singing
syncopation
vowels

VOICING
Two part

PERFORMANCE STYLE
With joy
Accompanied by keyboard
Trumpet optional

FOCUS
- Read and clap patterns with syncopation. ♪ ♩ ♪
- Sing with clear diction.
- Read and sing in two independent parts.

Warming Up

Rhythm Drill
Echo these rhythm patterns, then read them through until you can perform them correctly. Notice the syncopated rhythm ♪ ♩ ♪, a short-long-short organization of sounds.

Vocal Warm-Up
Sing each of these patterns on solfège and hand signs, continuing up by half steps on each repeat. Try to memorize the interval sounds. On another day, use *lay*, *lee*, *lie*, *low*, or *loo* to practice forming pure vowel sounds.

Sight-Singing

First clap the rhythm of each part. Then sight-sing each line of this exercise using solfège and hand signs or numbers. Finally sing the exercise in two parts. Notice when the parts move from unison to two different parts.

Singing: "Lift Up Your Voice, Alleluia"

If you want to be understood, you need to know your message and speak it clearly. Read the text of "Lift Up Your Voice, Alleluia." What is the mood? How do you know? Say the text of measures 15–22 with a locked jaw. Now repeat them with clear diction, forming the vowels clearly, and moving your jaw as much as possible.

Now turn to the music for "Lift Up Your Voice, Alleluia" on page 12.

HOW DID YOU DO?

?

As you continue your journey of vocal development and part singing, think about your preparation and performance of "Lift Up Your Voice, Alleluia."
1. Can you read and perform the rhythm accurately?
2. Describe syncopated rhythm.

3. Explain how you can be sure your diction is understood.
4. How well were you able to sing in two parts? What was easy? What was difficult?
5. Compare your ability to the ability level of your group. What can you do better? How can you help out?

Lift Up Your Voice, Alleluia

Words and Music by
Sally K. Albrecht

Two-part Voices and Keyboard with Optional Trumpet*

*Trumpet Part is located on Page 11.

11348

lu - ia; ___ Raise your song to the glo - ri - ous sky. ___

Lift up your voice, al - le - lu - ia; ___ Praise to the heav'ns on

high. Sing al - le - lu - ia; ___

15 PART I (or unis.)
mf

mf

11348

Raise your song to the glo-ri-ous sky. __ Sing al-le-

lu - ia; __ Praise to the heav'ns on high.

11348

11348

*Alternate Christmas text in italics.

11348

hearts and lives_ as we join_ in praise.
peace and joy,_ a star shows the way.

hearts and lives_ as we join_ in praise.
peace and joy,_ a star shows the way.

Lift up your voice, al- le- lu - ia;_ Raise your song to the

Lift up your voice, al- le- lu - ia;_ Raise your song to the

glo - ri - ous sky. _ Lift up your voice, al - le - lu - ia; _

glo - ri - ous sky. _ Lift up your voice, al - le - lu - ia; _

Praise to the heav'ns on high.

Praise to the heav'ns on high.

11348

Praise to the heav'ns on high.

Praise to the heav'ns on high.

Praise to the heav'ns on high.

11348

LESSON 3

No Well, No Well!

Based on Two Traditional Carols
COMPOSER: *Steve Kupferschmid*

CHORAL MUSIC TERMS
beat
breathing mechanics
compound meter
rhythm
6/8 meter

VOICING
Two part

PERFORMANCE STYLE
March tempo
Accompanied by piano

FOCUS
- Distinguish between beat and rhythm.
- Read and clap patterns in 6/8 meter.
- Identify and use proper breathing technique.

Warming Up

Rhythm Drill

In two groups, pat the beat and clap the rhythm. Then switch parts. Decide on other body percussion or vocal sound syllables to perform the beat and rhythm. The beat is divided into three parts. ♫♪; ♩ ♪; ♩. This is known as *compound meter*.

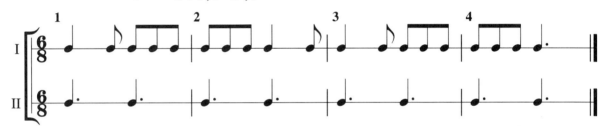

Vocal Warm-Up 1

Sing each of these patterns on solfège and hand signs or numbers, continuing up by half steps. Then sing this exercise on the syllable *doo*. Clap the beat indicated.

Continue up by half steps.

Clap:

Vocal Warm-Up 2

Sing the patterns on solfège or numbers. Add claps as you sing.

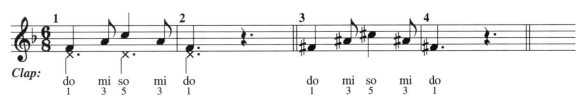

Clap:

Vocal Warm-Up 3

Memorize the sounds of the intervals in this exercise. Continue up by half steps.

Sight-Singing

First clap the rhythm of each part. Identify the solfège pitches. Then sight-sing each line of this exercise using solfège and hand signs or numbers. Finally, sing the exercise in two parts. Breathe correctly at the beginning and before the second phrase.

Singing: "No Well, No Well!"

Your breath is the foundation of your singing. Although music is an art, correct breathing is a practiced skill. Controlling your breathing will allow you to sing through long, flowing phrases. Stand, demonstrating good posture—relaxed shoulders, backbone straight, rib cage high, and head held level. Inhale four counts; hold four counts; exhale four counts with a "hiss." Now repeat with eight counts per step, then 16. Keep your shoulders down as you inhale.

Now turn to the music for "No Well, No Well!" on page 23.

HOW DID YOU DO?

?

?

Think about your preparation and performance of "No Well, No Well!"
1. Can you read and perform the rhythm accurately? What is easy or difficult about reading 6/8 rhythms?
2. Describe the difference between beat and rhythm.
3. Describe some characteristics of proper breathing technique.

4. Choose a section of "No Well, No Well!" Perform it with a classmate to demonstrate either beat and rhythm, 6/8 meter, or proper breathing. Maybe your performance will demonstrate all three. Describe what you are demonstrating before you begin.
5. What do you like about "No Well, No Well!"? What would you change?

No Well, No Well!

(Bring Some Water, Jeannette, Isabella!)

By Steve Kupferschmid (ASCAP)

Two-part Voices and Piano*

No well, no well, no well!

Bring some wa - ter, Jean - nette, Is - a - bel - la!

* Also available for S.A.T.B. (4767) and 3-part mixed voices (4768).

4769

Field and prai - rie make us ver - y thirst - y for a
Humps are sag - ging, tongues are drag - ging, thirst - y for a

Field and prai - rie make us ver - y thirst - y for a
Humps are sag - ging, tongues are drag - ging, thirst - y for a

jar of wa - ter. But there is no
jar of wa - ter. We will soon go

jar of wa - ter.
jar of wa - ter.

well a - round. No -
up in smoke.

There's no wa - ter to be found.
We would set - tle for a Coke.

4769

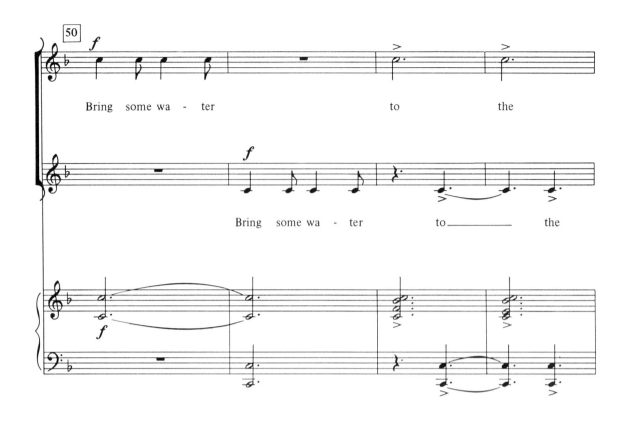

Bring some wa - ter   to   the

Bring some wa - ter   to _____ the

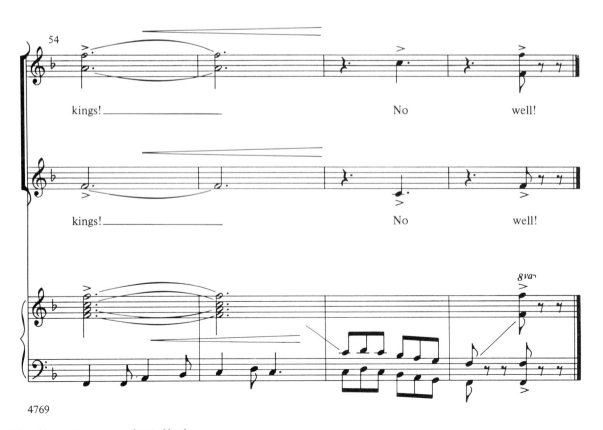

kings! _____   No   well!

kings! _____   No   well!

LESSON 4

Peace in Twelve Languages

CHORAL MUSIC TERMS
expressive singing
tie
tonic triad

COMPOSER: *Thomas Knight*
ARRANGER: *Craig Palmer*

VOICING
Two part

PERFORMANCE STYLE
Smoothly, with feeling
Accompanied by piano
Optional flute

FOCUS
- Read and clap rhythms with ties.
- Recognize, read, and sing the tonic triad.
- Sing expressively.

Warming Up

Rhythm Drills

Read and clap Rhythm Drill I. Now look at Rhythm Drill II. How are they different? How differently do you think they will sound? Read and clap Rhythm Drill II until it feels comfortable.

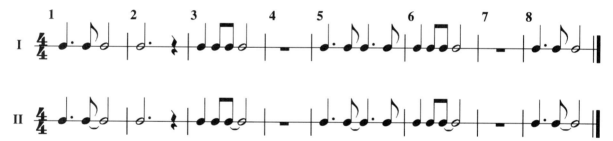

Vocal Warm-Up 1

Sing this exercise, first with *hah*, then using solfège and hand signs or numbers. The pitches *do*, *mi*, and *so* make up the tonic triad.

*Continue up
by half steps.*

do mi so mi do
1 3 5 3 1

do mi so mi do
1 3 5 3 1

Vocal Warm-Up 2

Echo sing each pattern using solfège and hand signs or numbers. Start with just measure **a.** and **b.**, then add one measure at a time, learning the new hand signs and pitches. Try to learn the sounds of the pitches in relation to one another.

Sight-Singing

Sight-sing each part with solfège and hand signs or numbers, then put the two together. Use your memory of pitches in the tonic chord to tune each pitch.

Singing: "Peace in Twelve Languages"

There are many ways to express your thoughts. Say "hello" in several different ways. What made each one different? How do the differences affect the meaning? How many ways do you know to say "peace"?

Now turn to the music for "Peace in Twelve Languages" on page 31.

HOW DID YOU DO?
?

You are learning many ways to make your singing more expressive. Think about your preparation and performance of "Peace in Twelve Languages."
1. Describe how a tie changes the rhythm.
2. What pitches make up the tonic triad? Can you sing them?

3. Create two different echo patterns using pitches of the tonic triad.
4. Do you think the composer did a good job of matching the idea of this text with the music he wrote? Give specific reasons why or why not.

Peace in Twelve Languages

Words and Music by
Thomas Knight
Arranged by Craig Palmer

Two-part, Accompanied
(with optional flute part)

Paz paix___ peace

Paz paix___ peace

8808

8808

hei – wa__ hoa bihn.

hei – wa__ hoa bihn.

25

Paz paix__ peace an - sio - chain__

Paz paix__ peace an - sio - chain__

frie - de__ sha - lom sa - laam__

frie - de__ sha - lom sa - laam__

8808

8808

Pax paix peace to you.

Pax paix peace to you.

D.S. al Coda

D.S. al Coda

8808

PRONUNCIATION GUIDE

Paz ("poz")	Spanish
Paix ("pay")	French
Peace	English
An ("on")	Korean
Siochan ("sha-kan")	Gaelic
Friede ("free-day")	German
Shalom	Hebrew
Salaam ("sa-lam")	Arabic
Irene ("ear-ree-knee")	Greek
Santeepop	Thai
Heiwa ("hey-wha")	Japanese
Hoa Bihn ("hwha-bin")	Vietnamese

8808

LESSON 5

Sing a Joyful Song

COMPOSER: Sally K. Albrecht

CHORAL MUSIC TERMS

articulation

legato

marcato

style

vowels

VOICING

Two part

PERFORMANCE STYLE

With majesty
Accompanied by keyboard
Trumpets optional

FOCUS

- Read and sing in tune pitches below *do*.
- Demonstrate marcato and legato articulation.
- Sing with correct vowel diction.

Warming Up

Vocal Warm-Up 1

Sing this exercise using solfège and hand signs or numbers. Listen carefully to the pitches below *do*. Go up a half step on each repeat. On another day, sing the exercise using vowel sounds: *na, ne, ni, no,* or *nu.*

Continue up by half steps.

| do | ti | la | so | do |
| 1 | 7 | 6 | 5 | 1 |

Vocal Warm-Up 2

Sing these pitches slowly using solfège and hand signs or numbers. Strive to secure the sound of each pitch in relationship to others. Isolate the difficult intervals and practice them until they become familiar.

do   so   do   so fa so
1   5   1   5   4   5

Sight-Singing

Identify the solfège, then sight-sing both parts using hand signs or numbers. Sing the exercise *marcato*, then *legato*.

Singing: "Sing a Joyful Song"

Get into style! Sing "Happy Birthday." Now change the style—sing it like a famous opera singer. Sing it like a rock star, then like a country star. How was each style different from the others?

Now turn to the music for "Sing a Joyful Song" on page 39.

HOW DID YOU DO?

You know a lot about style, and here's your chance to show it! Think about your preparation and performance of "Sing a Joyful Song."
1. Sing the pitches from low *so* up to *do* using solfège and hand signs.

2. Choose a phrase from this lesson and demonstrate the difference between marcato and legato articulation.
3. How do you form vowels correctly? Demonstrate.
4. What did you learn to do in this lesson that helps you create a style?

Sing a Joyful Song

Words and Music by
Sally K. Albrecht

Two-part Voices and Keyboard with Optional Trumpets*

Sing a joy-ful song, sing a hymn of praise. Sing a joy-ful song, let your voic-es raise.

Al-le-lu-ia, Al-le-lu - ia. Sing a joy-ful song, sing a hymn of praise.

*Trumpet parts are located on pages 10 and 11.

7932

A joy-ful song to the earth and the sky.   A joy-ful song, lift your
*A joy-ful song to the new-born King.   A joy-ful song, let your

A joy-ful song to the earth and the sky.   A joy-ful song, lift your
*A joy-ful song to the new-born King.   A joy-ful song, let your

voic - es high! _____
voic - es ring! _____

voic - es high! _____
voic - es ring! _____

* Alternate Christmas text in italics.

7932

7932

7932

Kwanzaa

COMPOSER: *Teresa Jennings*

CHORAL MUSIC TERMS
chord
improvisation
Kwanzaa

VOICING
Four part

PERFORMANCE STYLE
African beat, shuffle feel
Accompanied by piano
Percussion optional

FOCUS
• Read and sing one part independently from notation on one and two staves.
• Sing one pitch of a chord in tune.
• Improvise a rhythmic accompaniment.

Warming Up

 Vocal Warm-Up 1

Sing this exercise using solfège and hand signs or numbers. Then sing it in a canon after two beats. Try the canon singing on the vowel *oo*.

Continue up by half steps.

 Vocal Warm-Up 2

Find Part I and Part II. Read these pitches using solfège and hand signs or numbers. Notice that Part I has an extra note. When you get to the end, hold your last note, and you will have the first pitches for Vocal Warm-Up 3. This lesson outlines the tonic triad that you learned in Lesson 4.

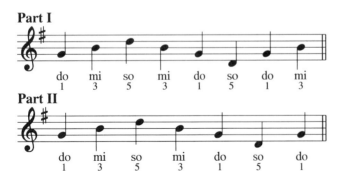

Part I

do mi so mi do so do mi
1 3 5 3 1 5 1 3

Part II

do mi so mi do so do
1 3 5 3 1 5 1

Vocal Warm-Up 3

Use the last pitch you sang in Vocal Warm-Up 2 to find your starting pitch. Sing this exercise in two parts. Listen carefully for in-tune singing and blend.

Sight-Singing

Identify the solfège or number of each note, sing the tonic triad to find your pitch, then sight-sing all three parts using hand signs. If necessary, sing each part separately first, then put them together.

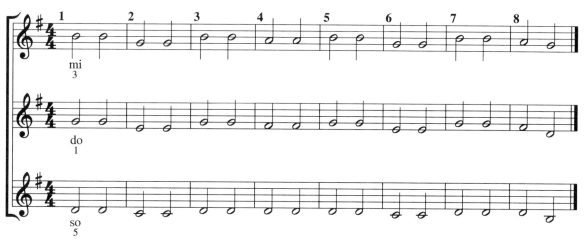

Singing: "Kwanzaa"

What is Kwanzaa? Tell the class anything you know about Kwanzaa. Read information about Kwanzaa to learn more about the celebration. Learn the melody and define the Swahili words in "Kwanzaa."

Now turn to the music for "Kwanzaa" on page 48.

HOW DID YOU DO?

During this lesson, you demonstrated several of the seven principles of Kwanzaa. Think about your preparation and performance of "Kwanzaa."

1. How well were you able to read and sing your part independently? Describe what you did well, and where you could improve. What principle were you working on?

2. Did your choir sing the chords in tune? How do you know? What principle were you demonstrating?

3. Describe how to improvise a rhythmic accompaniment. What principle do you demonstrate when you improvise?

4. Is "Kwanzaa" an appropriate song for the holiday? Why?

Kwanzaa

Words and Music by
Teresa Jennings

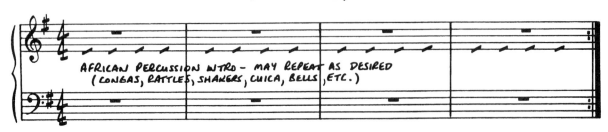

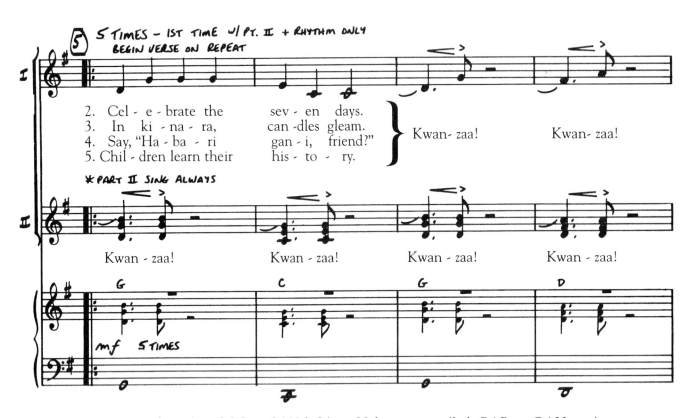

- nguzo saba = (nn-GOO-zo SAH-bah)
- kinara = (kee-NAH-rah)
- Habari gana = (hah-BAR-ee GAH-nee)
- Harambee = (hah-rahm-BEH)
- zawadi = (zah-WAH-dee)

* Opt. - sing top note only, or top 2 notes only

NOTE: By changing the shuffle feel to straight 8th notes, you can slow down or simplify the percussion parts.

With n-gu-zo sa-ba ways.
Light them, black and red and green.
Say, "Ha-ram-bee!" once a-gain.
Then, za-wa-di they re-ceive.

Kwan-zaa! Kwan-zaa!

Kwan-zaa! Kwan-zaa! Kwan-zaa! Kwan-zaa!

SOLO OR GROUP: SING EVERY TIME

Oh._____ Oh._____

BIG BREATH

Kwan-zaa! Kwan-zaa! Kwan-zaa! Kwan-zaa!

We Sing Feliz Navidad

CHORAL MUSIC TERMS

calypso style

harmony in thirds

improvisation

syncopated rhythm

COMPOSER: *Carl Strommen*

VOICING

Two part or SSA

PERFORMANCE STYLE

Light calypso syncopated rhythm

Accompanied by piano

FOCUS

- Read syncopated calypso rhythms.
- Identify and sing harmony in thirds.
- Improvise syncopated calypso rhythms.

Warming Up

Rhythm Drill

Echo clap these rhythms. They have syncopation in calypso style. Repeat each rhythm several times until it you are comfortable with it. Then clap the rhythms one after the other in different combinations.

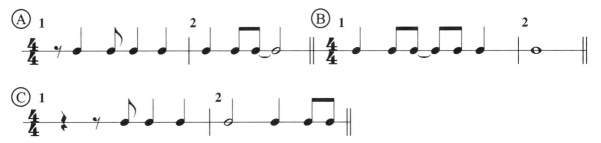

Vocal Warm-Up

Sing this Warm-Up using solfège and hand signs or numbers. This exercise has intervals of a third between the two parts. To find your beginning pitches, sing the tonic triad as you did in Vocal Warm-Up 2 in Lesson 6 page 46. Repeat the exercise, moving up stepwise on each repeat.

Sight-Singing

Clap the rhythm of your part. Then identify the solfège and sight-sing with solfège and hand signs or numbers. Notice the sound of harmony in thirds.

Singing: "We Sing Feliz Navidad"

What do you know about calypso music?

What does it sound like? Where does it come from? What do you know about the climate and scenery of this place? Close your eyes and imagine that you are there!

Now turn to the music for "We Sing Feliz Navidad" on page 53.

HOW DID YOU DO?

Just like calypso style allows each person to add his or her own ideas, you have added to your musical knowledge and skills. Think about your preparation and performance of "We Sing Feliz Navidad."

1. Describe how syncopated rhythms work, and clap the Rhythm Drill to demonstrate.

2. In a group of two or four, sing a part of "We Sing Feliz Navidad" that demonstrates harmony in thirds.

3. Explain how good you think you are at improvising syncopated calypso rhythms.

4. What do you like about this piece? If you could change it, would there be anything you would do differently?

We Sing Feliz Navidad

Words and Music by
Carl Strommen

Two-part/SSA Voices and Piano

11368

a Mer - ry Christ - mas to you.___ We bring Fe - liz Na - vi-dad___

a Mer - ry Christ - mas to you.___ We bring Fe - liz Na - vi-dad___

to one and all. La la la la la la la___

to one and all. La la la la la la la___

la la la la la la la,___ We bring Fe - liz Na - vi-dad___

la la la la la la la,___ We bring Fe - liz Na - vi-dad___

to one and all.

to one and all.

decresc.

43

mp

Sway - ing palms and shin - ing lights,_ sil - ver stars and South - ern nights,_

mp

Sway - ing palms and shin - ing lights,_ sil - ver stars and South - ern nights,_

mp

47

gen - tle breez-es soft - ly sing,_ there's Christ-mas in ___ the air.

gen - tle breez-es soft - ly sing,_ there's Christ-mas in ___ the air.

11368

In the Meadow

Hungarian Folk Song
ARRANGER: *Beatrice P. Krone*
TRANSLATOR: *Irene Bonyay Palotay*

CHORAL MUSIC TERMS

major triad

minor mode

minor triad

si

sixteenth notes

VOICING

SA

PERFORMANCE STYLE

Gaily

Accompanied by piano

FOCUS

- Read rhythms with sixteenth notes.
- Read and sing in E minor, including *si*.

Warming Up

 Rhythm Drill

Echo clap each rhythm pattern, then clap it until you are comfortable with it. Notice the sixteenth notes. Now clap all the patterns in order. Cover one measure at a time until you can clap the whole rhythm from memory.

 Vocal Warm-Up 1

Sing this pattern with solfège and hand signs or numbers. Now hand sign every pitch, but only sing the first and then every other pitch (1st, 3rd, 5th, and so on).

 Vocal Warm-Up 2

La, *do*, and *mi* build the *minor triad*. Sing them as a melody, then as a chord. Then immediately sing the *major triad*, *do*, *mi*, and *so*.

Vocal Warm-Up 3

Echo each pattern with solfège and hand signs or numbers. Notice the raised *so* to *si*. After each pattern is comfortable, sing the patterns in different orders, for example: a b c, b a c, or c b a.

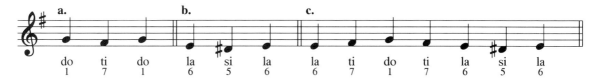

do ti do   la si la   la ti do ti la si la
1   7   1   6   5   6   6   7   1   7   6   5   6

Sight-Singing

Identify the solfège syllables, then sing with solfège and hand signs or numbers.

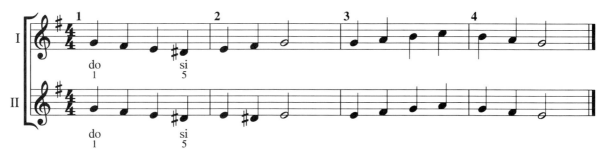

do   si
1   5

do   si
1   5

Singing: "In the Meadow"

At harvest time in Hungary, young men and women work very hard. They think ahead to the end of the harvest, when they can spend more time with one another.

Read the text of "In the Meadow." Which parts express the boy's and girl's ideas?

Now turn to the music for "In the Meadow" on page 62.

HOW DID YOU DO? ❓

Think about your preparation and performance of "In the Meadow."
1. Think about how you read the pitches and rhythms. Identify your strengths and weaknesses.

2. Describe what is meant by the common eighth note value in changing meters.
3. Explain how minor is different than major.

In the Meadow

Hungarian Folksong
Arranged by Beatrice P. Krone
First stanza
Adapted from the translation of Irene Bonyay Palotay by B.P.K.

SA Accompanied

Ed. 6120

Used with permission 1995/96.

Soon we'll join, we'll join in hap-py dance and song!

hard and long. Soon I'll join my sweet-heart in a dance and song, dance and song!

cresc.

Ap - ples round, and red and ver - y juic - y sweet; But with

Ap - ples round, red and ver - y juic - y sweet; But with

(faster)

her no sweet red ap - ples can com - pete! No! No! No!

her no sweet red ap - ples can com - pete! No! No! No!

Ed. 6120

LESSON

Dear Nightingale, Awake

Christmas Carol (1670)
ARRANGER: *Gerhard Track*
TRANSLATOR: *Gladys Wilson*

CHORAL MUSIC TERMS
German text
imitative parts
independence

VOICING
SA

PERFORMANCE STYLE
Allegro, happily
Accompanied by piano

FOCUS
- Read and sing in G major using solfège.
- Sing independently one of two parts, including imitative sections.
- Sing in German.

Warming Up

Rhythm Drill
Read and clap this Rhythm Drill. Watch out for the changes in meter. Keep the eighth note constant and you will be fine.

Vocal Warm-Up
Melodies have steps or skips. Look at each pattern and notice the interval that is labeled. Echo each pattern, then sing it several times until you have memorized the sound of the intervals.

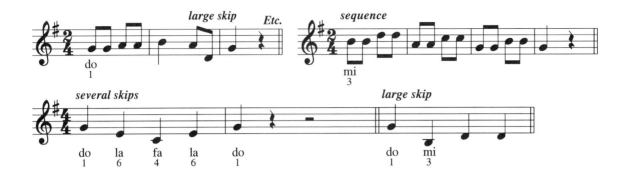

 ### Sight-Singing

Identify the solfège syllables or numbers of each note, then sing with solfège and hand signs or numbers. Try having the alto part begin one measure after the soprano part. Notice how the alto part imitates the soprano part.

 ## Singing: "Dear Nightingale, Awake"

If you were living with a family who did not speak your language at all, how would you communicate?

If you could speak a little of their language, what would you do to make sure you were clearly understood? Echo the pronunciation of the German text of "Dear Nightingale, Awake" being sure you are clearly understood.

Now turn to the music for "Dear Nightingale, Awake" on page 67.

<table>
<tr><td>HOW DID YOU DO?</td><td>If you start with an exciting, challenging piece, it can become an exciting performance for an audience. Think about your preparation and performance of "Dear Nightingale, Awake."

1. Describe your ability to sight-sing rhythms and pitches. What do you do well? What do you need to work on?</td><td>2. Choose a phrase to sing with a classmate demonstrating independent singing.
3. Listen to a classmate sing a phrase in German and give a critique. Tell what was good, and what can be improved.</td></tr>
</table>

Dear Nightingale, Awake

Christmas Carol (1670)
Arranged by Gerhard Track
Translated by Gladys Wilson

Christmas Chorus, SA Accompanied

224-4

sing the Ho—ly— Child is here! Fly hith-er to the
sing dem sar - ten Je - su-lein! Flieg' her sum Kripp-lein

Child, the Ho—ly— Child is here! Fly hith-er to the
Je - su - lein, dem Je - su-lein! Flieg' her sum Kripp-lein

crib,————— fly hith - er all the feath - ered kin, Let
klein,————— flieg her, ge - fie - dert Schwes - ter - lein, lass

crib,————— fly hith - er all the feath - ered kin, Let
klein,————— flieg her, ge - fie - dert Schwes - ter - lein, lass

pur - est tones pour from your throats, Sing— Night - in - gale so
tö - nen hold dein Schnä - be - lein, Sing Nach - ti - gall, gar

pur - est tones pour from your throats, Sing Night - in - gale so
tö - nen hold dein Schnä - be - lein, Sing Nach - ti - gall, gar

LESSON 10

The First Noel/ Pachelbel's Canon

CHORAL MUSIC TERMS

andante

ostinato

phrase

repetition

tie

variation

Traditional English Carol and Canon in D
COMPOSER: *Johann Pachelbel* (1653–1706)
ARRANGER: *Michael Clawson*

VOICING

SSA

PERFORMANCE STYLE

Andante
Accompanied by piano (two players) or organ

FOCUS

- Read and clap rhythms with ties.
- Recognize and describe repetition and variation.
- Sing independently one of two parts over an ostinato accompaniment.
- Identify phrases and sing with natural phrase breaks.

Warming Up

Rhythm Drill

Read and clap this Rhythm Drill. Compare patterns I and II. How are they the same, and how are they different?

Vocal Warm-Up

Sing the tonic triad as notated below. Then sing the familiar melody at the top of page 72. Sing it using solfège and hand signs or numbers, but be careful! It has a surprise!

Sight-Singing

Identify the solfège syllables, then sight-sing with solfège and hand signs or numbers. Find your beginning pitch from the tonic triad. Sing one part at a time, then put the two parts together.

Singing: "The First Noel/Pachebel's Canon"

One of the mysteries of music is that both repetition and contrast provide interest.

Listen to the bass line of the piano part all the way through "The First Noel/Pachelbel's Canon." If you can find the pattern, sing along in your own range. You will be surprised at the importance of this simple repeated phrase.

Now turn to the music for "The First Noel/Pachelbel's Canon" on page 73.

HOW DID YOU DO?

If you start with an exciting, challenging piece, it can become an exciting performance for an audience. Think about your performance of "The First Noel/ Pachelbel's Canon."

1. Define *ostinato* and tell where you can find one in the music.

2. Describe two ways that the arranger varied "The First Noel" for this composition.

3. Choose a section of the piece to sing with a few classmates to show your skill at singing independently in two parts. Sing with words or solfège.

4. Do you think it is acceptable to change a traditional carol to fit the accompaniment? Why or why not?

To Cindy, Matthew, and Brandon.
Merry Christmas

The First Noel/Pachelbel's Canon

Traditional English Carol *and* Canon in D *by*
Johann Pachelbel (1653–1706)
Arranged by Michael Clawson

SSA Voices and Piano (two players) or Organ

The_

7753

first _____ No - el, the _ an - gel did say, _____ Was to

cer - tain poor shep - herds in fields as they lay.

In _

fields _____ where they lay_ keep - ing their sheep, _____ On a

cold win - ter's night _____ that was _____ so deep. No -

No -

No -

29

el, _____ No - el, No - el, _____ No - el. _____

el, No - el, No - el, No - el, No - el. _____

mf

mf

33

f

Born   is   the   King _____ of   Is - ra - el.

f

Born   is   the   King _____ of   Is - ra - el. _____ No -

f

f

37

No - el,   No - el,   No - el,   No - el, No -

el,   No - el,   No - el, _____ No - el,   No -

41

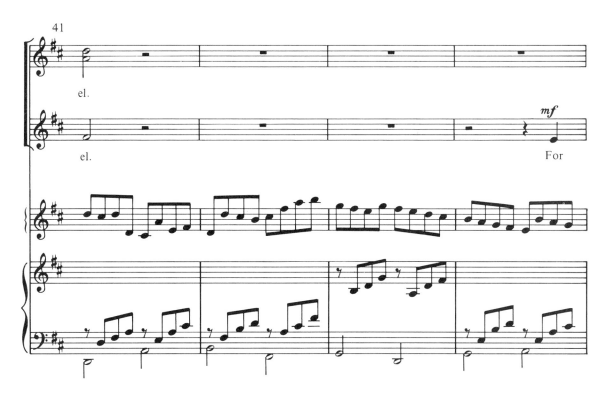

el.

el.   For

all to see there was a star___ shin - ing in the east be - yond them

far. And to ___ the ___ earth it gave ___ great ___ light and it con - tin - ued

And to ___ the ___ earth it gave ___ great ___ light, light both

day   and _____   night.

day _____   and   night.

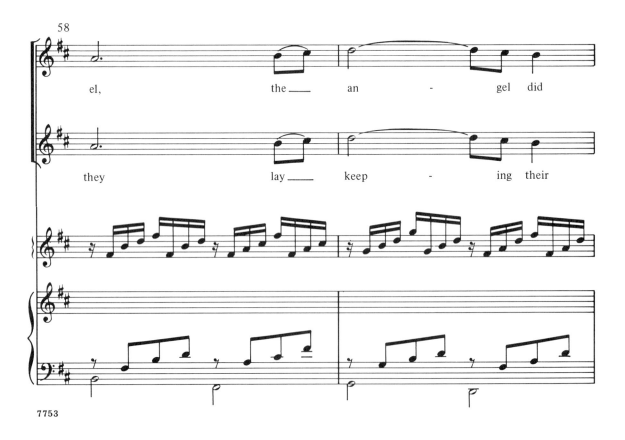

say, _____ Was to cer - tain poor

sheep, _____ On a cold win - ter's

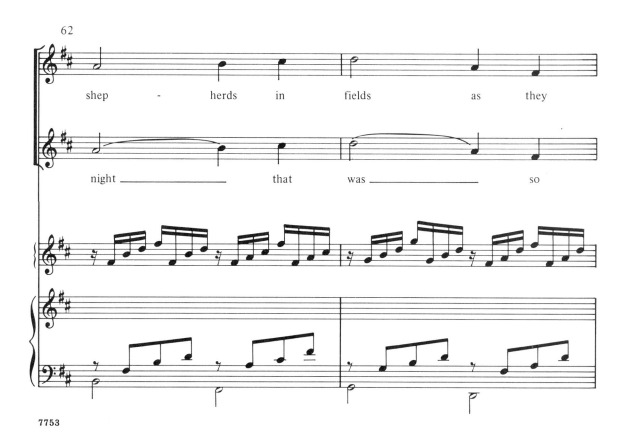

shep - herds in fields as they

night _____ that was _____ so

The First Noel/Pachelbel's Canon **81**

7753

Born is the King _____ of Is - ra - el.

Born is the King _____ of Is - ra - el. _____ No -

No - el, No - el, No - el, No - el, No - el.

el, No - el, No - el, _____ No - el, No - el.

Annabel Lee

COMPOSERS: *Edna Lewis* and *John Mitri Habash*
TEXT: *Edgar Allan Poe* (1809–1849)

CHORAL MUSIC TERMS
expressive singing, mood
fermata
part independence
voice crossing

VOICING
SSA

PERFORMANCE STYLE
Moderately slow
Accompanied by piano

FOCUS
- Read and sing in G minor.
- Identify and sing expressively to convey mood.
- Sing independently one of three parts with voice crossing.

Warming Up

Vocal Warm-Up
Sing this exercise using solfège and hand signs or numbers. Choose a mood and convey it as you sing. Describe how you changed your sound.

Sight-Singing
Identify the solfège syllables, then sight-sing with solfège and hand signs or numbers. Sing one part at a time, then put the two parts together. Now add the third part. Where do the parts cross?

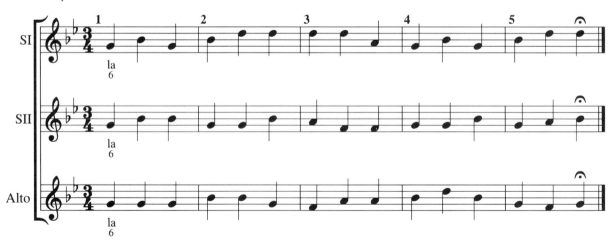

Singing: "Annabel Lee"

When words alone are not enough to convey a mood, people turn to music.

Read the text of "Annabel Lee." What is the overall mood of the poem? Describe the mood of each verse, listing your descriptions in order on the chalkboard.

Now turn to the music for "Annabel Lee" on page 86.

HOW DID YOU DO?

?

You can create a tragic mood and still have a triumphant performance. Think about your preparation and performance of "Annabel Lee."

1. Discuss the mood of the piece, and how you created that mood musically.

2. Describe and demonstrate voice crossing with two classmates.

3. Was the mood of "Annabel Lee" effectively communicated through the music by the composers? How?

4. Listen to your performance of "Annabel Lee" and critique it for effective communication of mood.

Annabel Lee

Words and Music by
Edna Lewis and John Mitri Habash
Adapted from Edgar Allan Poe (1809–1849)

Three-part, SSA

AMI 013-7

watched their love in fear and jeal - ous - y. _____

watched their love in fear and jeal - ous - y. _____

watched their love in fear and jeal - ous - y. _____

Dm   Gm   Dm

D

_____ Sent a wick - ed wind to kill

_____ Sent a wick - ed wind to kill

_____ Sent a wick - ed wind to kill

D

Gm   Dm

beau - ti - ful An - na - bel Lee. _____

beau - ti - ful An - na - bel Lee. _____

beau - ti - ful An - na - bel Lee. _____

E♭   Dm7   G   cresc.   Gm

AMI 013-7

AMI 013-7

A la Nanita Nana

Mexican Folk Song
ARRANGER: *David Eddleman*

CHORAL MUSIC TERMS

lullaby

parallel minor

Spanish triplet

VOICING

Two-part choir

PERFORMANCE STYLE

Tenderly

Accompanied by keyboard

FOCUS

- Describe the relationship between minor and parallel major.
- Read and sing in D minor and D major.
- Sing with correct Spanish pronunciation.
- Identify characteristics of a lullaby.
- Identify some characteristics of Spanish music.

Warming Up

Rhythm Drill

This rhythm, the Spanish triplet, is characteristic of Spanish music. Practice it slowly, then speed it up.

dee   dee del di da

Vocal Warm-Up

Sing this exercise slowly using solfège and hand signs or numbers. Notice that the major and minor keys begin on the same pitch. These are called *parallel major and minor.*

*Continue up
by half steps.*

Minor: la ti do re mi
6 7 1 2 3

Major: do re mi fa so
1 2 3 4 5

Sight-Singing

Identify the solfège syllables, then sing with solfège and hand signs or numbers. Describe the relationship between D minor and D major. How are they the same? How are they different?

Singing: "A la Nanita Nana"

When you hear the word "lullaby" certain characteristics come to mind. What characteristics do you think a lullaby should have? Why?

Now turn to the music for "A la Nanita Nana" on page 95.

HOW DID YOU DO?

? ?

Even though "A la Nanita Nana" is a lullaby, you can't sleep through the performance! Think about your preparation and performance of "A la Nanita Nana."
1. Describe the use of major and minor, and the effect.
2. Sing the Sight-Singing exercise to demonstrate your ability to read in major and minor.

3. How was your Spanish pronunciation? Choose and perform part of the piece that you think you do well.
4. Do you think "A la Nanita Nana" is an effective lullaby? Why?
5. Describe the characteristics of Spanish music that appear in "A la Nanita Nana."

A la Nanita Nana

(Murm'ring a Lullaby)

Mexican Folk Song
Arranged by David Eddleman
English version: David Eddleman

Two-part Choir of Treble Voices with Keyboard

CM8303

CM8303

na - na, na - ni - ta   ¡e - a!   Mi   Je - sus tie - ne   sue - ño ¡ben-di - to,
low - ly, sing soft - ly   e - a,   See   how my child is   sleep - ing in ho - ly

na - na,   na - ni - ta   ¡e - a!   ¡Ben -
by,   soft - ly sing e - a,   Oh,

ben - di - to___   se - a!_____
slum - ber,___ blest___   ba - by._____

di - to___   se - a!_____
bless - ed   ba - by._____

unison chorus   mf dolce
                 Fuen - te - ci - lla que co - rre   cla - ra y   so -
                 Foun - tain is run-ning clear - ly,   laugh - ing   and

mf legato e dolce

CM8303

CM8303

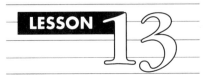

LESSON 13

For the Beauty of the Earth

CHORAL MUSIC TERMS

al fine

delicato

dolce

espressione (espress.)

legato

mezzo forte (mf)

mezzo piano (mp)

rallentando (rall.)

unison

COMPOSER: *John Rutter*

TEXT: *F. S. Pierpoint* (1835–1917)

VOICING

Two-part choir

PERFORMANCE STYLE

Happily, legato, delicato

Accompanied by piano

FOCUS

• Flexible tone.

• Flexible syllabic stress.

Warming Up

Vocal Warm-Up 1

Sing this exercise, using solfège and hand signs or numbers. Remember to maintain good breath control and use well-articulated vowels on *so*, *la*, and *so*.

Continue up to the key of B♭.

Vocal Warm-Up 2

This warm-up will stretch your upper range into an open, free-flowing tone. Keep the energy and breath flowing on the highest note. Strive for a flexible tone, especially on the sixteenth notes and descending eighth notes.

Continue up by half steps.

yah hah hah hah   ah

Vocal Warm-Up 3

Sing using solfège and hand signs or numbers in two parts. Many two-part songs have intervals of thirds.

2.

Vocal Warm-Up 4

First say the rhythm, using the rhythm syllables. Then sing, using the rhythm syllables. Maintain the flexible, agile tone quality you achieved in Warm-Up 2.

ta   ti ki ta

Sight-Singing

Identify solfège, and sing using hand signs and syllables or numbers.

Singing: "For the Beauty of the Earth"

How many ways can you say, "How are you today?"

Try saying the phrase four times. Each time place the emphasis on a different word. For example: *How* are you today? How *are* you today? and so forth. Does the meaning change slightly with the change in emphasis?

Now turn to the music for "For the Beauty of the Earth" on page 104.

HOW DID YOU DO?

?

Do you enjoy the beauties of the earth? Have you ever watched a sunrise or looked closely at a flower? Think about your preparation and performance of "For the Beauty of the Earth."
1. Did your performance evoke the awe of natural wonders?

2. Were you able to maintain a flexible tone?
3. Was your syllabic stress flexible throughout?
4. How do you feel you did? Where could you improve? What did you do best?
5. How did the choir perform as a group?

Commissioned by the Texas Choral Director's Association

For the Beauty of the Earth

COMPOSER: John Rutter
Words by F. S. Pierpoint (1835–1917)

Two-part Choir SA, with Piano

This setting is scored for small orchestra (2 fl, 2 ob, 2 cl, bsn, 2 hn, perc, hp, strings).
Full score and parts are on rental from Hinshaw Music, Inc.

HMC-469

Reprinted by permission.

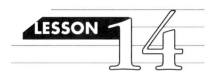
Joshua Fit the Battle of Jericho

CHORAL MUSIC TERMS
chord tones
spiritual

Traditional Spiritual
ARRANGER: *Warren Williamson*

VOICING

SSA

PERFORMANCE STYLE

Very lively
Accompanied by piano

FOCUS

- Read and sing in three parts, tuning chords in minor.
- Identify and sing in spiritual style.
- Assess your own performance.

Warming Up

Vocal Warm-Up 1

Sing this Warm-Up, using solfège or numbers. Repeat, moving up by half steps.

Vocal Warm-Up 2

First clap the rhythm. Next sing the solfège or numbers, tuning the chords carefully. Continue up by half steps. Finally, learn and add the step/clap pattern. Can you sing and do this pattern?

Sight-Singing

Read and sing this exercise using solfège and hand signs or numbers. Then sing it on *loo*, listening carefully to each other. Make each chord instantly tune up, until it becomes automatic.

 ## Singing: *"Joshua Fit the Battle of Jericho"*

What do you know about Joshua and the Battle of Jericho?

Who was Joshua? Where is Jericho? When was the battle? Where can you read this story?

HOW DID YOU DO?

?

Think about your preparation and performance of "Joshua Fit the Battle of Jericho."
1. Are you comfortable singing in minor? What can you do well? Where could you do better?
2. What does "spiritual style" suggest to you about the written notation?

3. How well did you perform "Joshua Fit the Battle of Jericho"? How well did the choir perform? What criteria did you use to make this evaluation?

Joshua Fit the Battle of Jericho

Traditional Spiritual
Edited and Arranged by Warren Williamson

For Treble Voices, SSA

LESSON 15

The Ash Grove

Welsh Folk Song
ARRANGER: Thurlow T. Steffy

CHORAL MUSIC TERMS
anacrusis (upbeat)
a tempo
chord tones
phrase
ritardando (rit.)
tuning

VOICING
SSA

PERFORMANCE STYLE
Moderate tempo
Accompanied by keyboard

FOCUS
- Perform correct phrasing.
- Identify anacrusis (upbeat notes).
- Sing in three parts, tuning chords.

Warming Up

Vocal Warm-Up

Sing this Warm-Up using solfège and hand signs or numbers. Sing again, showing arm arcs for each phrase. Notice that the phrases begin on the third beat of a measure. This is called an *anacrusis*, or upbeat.

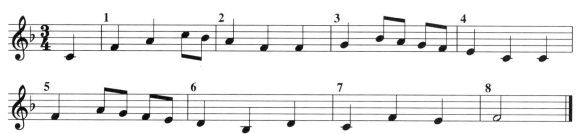

Sight-Singing

Read and sing this exercise using solfège and hand signs or numbers. Sing each line separately, then put the three parts together, singing slowly on *loo*, tuning each chord quickly. Does the last chord feel like an ending? Why?

Singing: "The Ash Grove"

Trees are an important element in our lives—improving our environment, and giving us food and products. They provide shade and beautiful scenery. Read the text of "The Ash Grove," then restate it in your own words. Does the text flow in short, choppy phrases or long flowing ones?

Now turn to the music for "The Ash Grove" on page 122.

HOW DID YOU DO?

?

The tree of knowledge and skill keeps growing each time you learn a new piece. Think about your preparation and performance of "The Ash Grove."
1. Describe the phrases in "The Ash Grove." Then sing a phrase, demonstrating your ability to sing it correctly.

2. Describe anacrusis.
3. How are your chords sounding? Do they tune quickly and well? Choose a phrase of "The Ash Grove" to sing with two classmates, to show how well you tune chords.

The Ash Grove

Welsh Folksong
Arranged by Thurlow T. Steffy

Three-part Treble Voices, with Keyboard Accompaniment

Making Historical Connections

▲ The *Madonna and Child* by Giovanni Bellini (c. 1430–1516) expresses a calm and idyllic mood. This mood is
similar to the quiet, devotional quality of Renaissance religious music.

c. 1470–75. Giovanni Bellini. *Madonna and Child*. Tempera and oil on wood panel. 82 x 58 cm (32³⁄₈ x 22³⁄₄"). Kimbell Art Museum, Fort Worth, Texas.

Renaissance Period

After completing this lesson, you should be able to:

- Describe the developments that took place in music during the Renaissance period.
- Compare the differences in sacred music between the Middle Ages and the Renaissance.
- Define madrigal, Renaissance, and polyphony.

Think of recent discoveries that have changed your life. Due to advances in technology and communications, you are living in a time of great change. Sophisticated computers and telecommunications systems affect how you receive and process information. Explorers are traveling into space and deep into the ocean. New scientific discoveries are making life better on Earth, and better *for* Earth. New art and music styles are being created. Some people say that we live in a very exciting time, because we are only now realizing the range of possibilities before us.

The Renaissance—a Time of Rebirth

The fifteenth and sixteenth centuries were a similar time in history. This period has become known as the **Renaissance,** which means *rebirth* or *renewal*. During the Renaissance period (c. 1430–1600), tremendous growth and discoveries took place. Great achievements occurred in music, art, and literature.

At the same time, explorers traveled to new continents and experienced very different cultures. Scientists such as Copernicus, Galileo, and da Vinci explored the idea that the Earth was not the center of everything, but perhaps revolved around the sun. In the early 1500s, the Protestant Reformation, led by Martin Luther, began and brought about other important developments in religion, politics, and music.

One of the most important contributions of the Renaissance, however, is attributed to Johann Gutenberg, who perfected the printing press in the mid-1400s. The invention of movable type accelerated opportunities to learn. Before that time, books were rare and expensive and had to be copied by hand. With the printing press came mass-produced books, and many more people were able to learn the arts of reading both words and music.

Looking Back

Most written music during the Middle Ages (eleventh to the fifteenth centuries) was composed for and performed in church. Many of the texts were taken mainly from the Book of Psalms

COMPOSERS

Guillaume Dufay (1400–1474)
Josquin Desprez (c. 1440–1521)
William Cornysh (c. 1465–1523)
Christopher Tye (c. 1500–c. 1572)
Giovanni Pierluigi da Palestrina (c. 1525–1594)
Orlando di Lasso (1532–1594)
William Byrd (c. 1543–1623)
Antonio Lotti (1667–1740)
Luca Marenzio (1553–1599)
John Farmer (c.1570–1601)
Michael Praetorius (c. 1571–1621)
Thomas Weelkes (1575–1623)

ARTISTS

Donatello (1386–1466)
Leonardo da Vinci (1452–1519)
Giovanni Bellini (c.1430–1516)
Michelangelo (1475–1564)
Raphael (1483–1520)
Titian (c.1488–1576)

AUTHORS

Martin Luther (1483–1546)
Sir Walter Raleigh (c. 1552–1618)
Sir Philip Sidney (1554–1586)
William Shakespeare (1564–1616)

CHORAL MUSIC TERMS

madrigal
polyphony
Renaissance
sacred music
secular music

Gutenberg press;
beginning of modern printing

c. 1435

Sistine Chapel construction begins

1473

Columbus lands in
West Indies/Americas

1492

1465

First printed music appears

1480

Sistine Chapel finished

in the Old Testament of the Bible. The music was chanted in unison in Latin, without accompaniment. This musical form is called Gregorian chant, and it marks the beginning of Western art music. Many of these chants, as well as popular folk melodies, became the basis for two-, three-, or four-part compositions. Since the voices used were of equal ranges and vocal quality, the sound of vocal groups during the Middle Ages lacked a full choral range. During the Middle Ages, however, scales, solfège, and the beginnings of musical notation were developed.

▲ **The artists and architects of the Renaissance rediscovered Classical antiquity and were inspired by what they found. In 1547, Michelangelo (1475–1564) became chief architect for the replacement of the original basilica of Old St. Peter's. Architect Giacomo della Porta finished the dome 26 years after Michelangelo's death.**

1546–64. Michelangelo. Exterior view, St. Peter's. St. Peter's Basilica, Vatican State, Rome, Italy. (Dome completed by Giacomo della Porta, 1590.)

Music and Art

The Renaissance was a time when scholars and artists became interested in the study of Greek and Roman art, architecture, and philosophy. The major artists of the period, such as Leonardo da Vinci, Raphael, Titian, Michelangelo, Bellini, and Donatello began to capture the new feeling of individuality and human achievement that was emerging. You will notice that their art celebrates the lifelike and realistic appearance of the individual.

New art and music styles emerged. **Sacred music,** or *hymns, chorales,* and *early masses,* also changed. Eventually, the equal-voice quality of the music of the Middle Ages developed into the full choral range of the present-day choir. Imitative forms continued to develop, with more and more independence of parts. Now the music could be printed, distributed, and read. Instruments such as organs, strings (lute and viol), and winds (recorder, shawm) began to be used with voices in processions and other ceremonies. Martin Luther believed that languages other than Latin were suitable for worship, so he translated the Bible into German. He then composed hymns in German so everyone could sing parts of the church services.

Magellan begins voyage around the world

1519

Composer William Byrd born

1543

1517

Protestant Reformation begins in Germany with Luther's 95 Theses

1584

Sir Walter Raleigh discovers Virginia

1522

Magellan's crew ends voyage around the world

Secular music, *any music that is not sacred*, also flourished during the Renaissance. For the first time in history, musicians traveled throughout Europe, bringing new styles from one country to another. Popular songs and madrigals were common and were frequently fused to create even newer styles. A **madrigal** is *a secular vocal form written in several imitative parts*. Each part is equally important, and the parts weave together to form polyphony. **Polyphony** means that *each voice part begins at a different place, is independent and important, and sections often repeat in contrasting dynamic levels* (poly—many, phony—sounds).

Choral music became more and more complex. Because more people were reading and singing composed songs, the range and depth of expression expanded. While polyphony existed during the Middle Ages, it was developed during the Renaissance, causing this period to frequently be called "the golden age of polyphony." People sang polyphony in church, at home, and for celebrations.

A Modern Renaissance

You also live in an age of great change, combined with tremendous possibilities. This time could be compared to that of the Renaissance. Perhaps your creativity and imagination will inspire you to be one of the new explorers, inventors, artists, or musicians who will discover new ways to look at the world.

Check Your Understanding

Recall

1. Describe some of the nonmusical changes that occurred during the Renaissance.

2. How did sacred music change from the Middle Ages to the Renaissance?

3. How did secular music change during the Renaissance?

4. Define a madrigal.

5. Describe polyphony.

Thinking It Through

1. Compare the influence of the printing press during the Renaissance to the development of the computer today. What modern changes are similar to the changes that occurred during the Renaissance?

2. What new skills did people need to learn in order to participate in music during the Renaissance?

Listening to...
Renaissance Music

CHORAL SELECTION

Farmer — "Fair Phyllis"

John Farmer (c. 1570–1601) was born in Dublin, Ireland. When he was 25 years old he was given the position of organist and choir master at Christ Church Cathedral in Dublin. Four years later he moved to London and published one collection of four-part madrigals. John Farmer was a contemporary of other madrigalists, two of whom were Thomas Weelkes (c. 1575–1623) and Thomas Morley (1557–1602). Certain influences of the other composers' works appear in the compositions of John Farmer.

"Fair Phyllis," with its fine texture and melancholy tone, is typical of the style of John Farmer. Its simple theme and liveliness has made it a popular English madrigal.

INSTRUMENTAL SELECTION

Anonymous — "Saltarello"

The word *saltarello* is a broad term for swift Italian folk dances. These dances involve jumping and are usually in triple meter. Generally, a saltarello consists of several repeated melodies with each melody having a different ending. The origin of these dances is unknown, but the earliest recorded use of saltarello as a musical term is in the late fourteenth and early fifteenth centuries. Saltarellos were popular throughout several different musical periods because of their authentic folk-dance quality.

RENAISSANCE CONNECTIONS

Introducing...
"Non Nobis, Domine"

William Byrd

Setting the Stage

"Non Nobis, Domine" is performed in Latin and sung a cappella as part of the Roman Catholic Church service. It was written as a canon (different from having a melody line and harmony lines). Therefore, it is polyphonic (several melodic lines moving at the same time). All voice parts are equal in importance. This is beautiful three-part piece full of rich musical sounds and complex harmonies. It will be appreciated by any audience.

Meeting the Composer
William Byrd (c.1543–1623)

William Byrd was one of the most famous and versatile English composers of the Renaissance. He wrote all styles of music. Although his compositions were religious in nature, he reached far beyond the already existing church music. He excelled in many kinds of chamber music: sacred and secular songs for domestic use and a variety of forms and styles which ranged from lullabies to theater music.

In 1575, Queen Elizabeth I granted Byrd and Tallis (Byrd's teacher) the exclusive rights to print, publish, import, and sell music to print. As a publisher, Byrd helped introduce Italian madrigals to England. He composed for both the Catholic and the Anglican church services, therefore using both the Latin and English texts.

Non Nobis, Domine

COMPOSER: *William Byrd* (1543–1623)

TEXT: *Jean Ashworth Bartle*

CHORAL MUSIC TERMS

crescendo

decresendo

imitative style

Latin

staggered entrances

stepwise melodic
    movement

VOICING

SSA

PERFORMANCE STYLE

Legato

A cappella

FOCUS

- Identify and sing a canon.
- Identify, read, and sing stepwise melodies.
- Sing with correct Latin pronunciation.

Warming Up

Rhythm Drill

Clap the following exercise. Notice the staggered entrances. Switch parts, so you get practice with all entrances. Say the rhythms using different combinations of consonants and vowels.

Vocal Warm-Up

Sing the D major scale up and down on *loo* without pausing. Now sing it in three parts, with each part beginning two beats after the previous voice. Notice the star (∗) that tells you when to start the canon. This is another way to show staggered entrances.

Sight-Singing

Read and sing this exercise using solfège and hand signs or numbers. Notice the natural sign in the fifth measure. This sign changes the directions you get from the key signature, but only to the end of that measure. Notice the stepwise melodic movement, and the effect of the few melodic leaps.

Singing: "Non Nobis, Domine"

During the Renaissance, there was great emphasis placed on the importance of individual expression .

"Non Nobis, Domine" was composed by William Byrd to be part of the Roman Catholic service. It is full of rich musical sounds and complex harmonies, resulting from a well-constructed canon. All voice parts have equal importance.

Look at "Non Nobis, Domine," and predict what the music will sound like, just by looking at the notation and using your knowledge of the Renaissance Period.

Now turn to the music for "Non Nobis, Domine" on page 134.

HOW DID YOU DO?

?
?

"Non Nobis, Domine" was written more than 400 years ago during the reign of England's Elizabeth I (1558–1603), yet it is still performed today. Think about your preparation and performance of "Non Nobis, Domine."

1. How do staggered entrances work in a canon? Do you need to have staggered entrances to have a canon?

2. Does stepwise melodic movement make sight-singing easy? Why?

3. How was your Latin pronunciation?

4. How does "Non Nobis, Domine" reflect the characteristics of the Renaissance period?

Non Nobis, Domine

William Byrd (1543–1623)
Edited by Jean Ashworth Bartle
Psalm 115:1

Treble Voices, Three-parts, A cappella

The dramatization observed in this sculpture, *The Ecstasy of St. Teresa* by Gianlorenzo Bernini (1598–1680), demonstrates the Baroque quest for expression and movement. Here the saint floats in space as she receives a vision of heaven. Such drama, movement, and tension are also qualities prominent in the music of the period.

1645–52. Gianlorenzo Bernini. *The Ecstasy of* St. *Teresa.* Marble. Life-size. Cornaro Chapel, Santa Maria della Vittoria, Rome, Italy.

Baroque Period

After completing this lesson, you should be able to:

- *Describe some development   that took place during the Baroque period.*
- *Identify some forms and characteristics of Baroque instrumental and vocal music.*
- *Compare characteristics of Baroque art, architecture, and music.*
- *Define oratorio, cantata, and opera.*

Imagine a plain, brick, rectangular building. Notice the plain door and windows. Now begin to create elaboration on the features of this building. Imagine a fancier door, decoration around the door, and ornate columns. Imagine tile work and mosaic patterns over the brick, creating a fancy exterior. Now go through the front door into the hallway to see the gold woodwork, high domed ceilings, and paintings covering the walls and ceilings. You are imagining a building from the **Baroque period** (1600–1750)—*the period of elaboration*. (**Baroque** comes from an Italian word meaning *rocky, irregular*.)

The Baroque Period—a Time of Elaboration

The Baroque period in music developed around 1600. It reached its height and ended with the death of Johann Sebastian Bach in 1750. During this period, Baroque artists and musicians had a style that characteristically had dramatic flair and dynamic movement. The *music became so elaborate toward the end of this period* (mid-1700s) that it was termed *Rococo*. (**Rococo** comes from a French term describing *a certain type of rock work*.)

Looking Back

The Renaissance was a period of change, during which there was an increased interest and involvement in cultural activities. The invention of the printing press created a society in which reading and writing were more widely known, and ideas began to be easily shared. Sacred music was written with the increased involvement of everyday people, and secular music began to emerge with strong melody lines.

Music of the Baroque

During the Baroque period, there was a strong desire to classify and assimilate all knowledge. The strength of the individual's spirit and will shaped a very emotional sense of splendor in the arts.

COMPOSERS

Claudio Monteverdi (1567–1643)
Arcangelo Corelli (1643–1713)
Henry Purcell (1659–1695)
Antonio Vivaldi (1678–1741)
Johann Sebastian Bach (1685–1750)
George Frideric Handel (1685–1759)

ARTISTS

El Greco (1541–1614)
Peter Paul Rubens (1577–1640)
Artemisia Gentileschi (c. 1597– c. 1651)
Gianlorenzo Bernini (1598–1680)
Rembrandt van Rijn (1606–1669)
Judith Leyster (1609–1660)

AUTHORS

John Donne (c.1573–1631)
Rene Descartes (1596–1650)
John Milton (1608–1674)
Molière (1622–1673)

CHORAL MUSIC TERMS

Baroque period
cantata
continuo
elaboration
improvised
opera
oratorio
Rococo

▲ **1607**
Jamestown, Virginia
established settlement

▲ **1618–1648**
Thirty Years' War

▲ **1636**
Harvard College
founded

▲ **1643–1715**
Reign of Louis XIV, King of France

▲ **1608**
Telescope invented

The music of the Baroque period reflected the elaborate attitudes of society. Compositions had a strong sense of movement, many times with a *continually moving bass line,* called **continuo.** Melodies were highly ornamental, and more ornamentations were often **improvised,** *invented on the spur of the moment,* during performances. Underneath all the fancy elaboration, however, remained the clear, classical, mathematically precise forms and thinking symbolized by the plain, brick rectangular building you imagined earlier in the example on page 137. The sense of symmetry and planning is clear in the music of the Baroque.

Instrumental Forms

The Baroque period brought about a great interest in instrumental music. Keyboard instruments were refined and elaborated upon, including the clavichord, harpsichord, and organ. The modern string family was dominant, and the trumpet was a favorite melody instrument in the orchestras of the day.

Many new forms of music were developed during the Baroque period. The *suite* usually consisted of several movements, sometimes specific dance rhythms,

▲ **The Baroque period, the period of elaboration, is evident in the detailed exterior of the Palace at Versailles. In 1661, France's King Louis XIV ordered architects to build him the largest, most elaborate palace in the world.**

1682. Louis Le Vau and Jules Hardoin-Mansart. The Cour d'honneur of the Castle at Versailles. Chateau, Versailles, France.

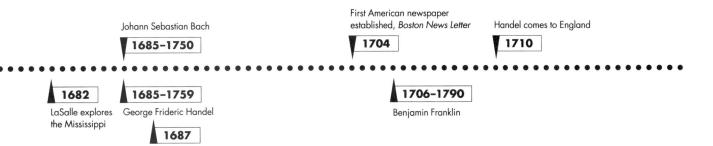

Johann Sebastian Bach

▼ 1685–1750

First American newspaper
established, *Boston News Letter*

▼ 1704

Handel comes to England

▼ 1710

▲ 1682
LaSalle explores
the Mississippi

▲ 1685–1759
George Frideric Handel

▲ 1706–1790
Benjamin Franklin

▲ 1687
Publication of Newton's *Mathematical Principles*

of contrasting tempos and styles. The *concerto grosso* was a form with several movements composed for a small chamber orchestra. The concerto grosso also contrasted a small musical group with the full orchestra. The pieces featured great clarity of parts, with a moving bass line and elaborate melody.

Vocal and Mixed Forms

Opera was born during the Baroque period, and is considered one of the most important vocal developments of the time. **Opera** is *a combination of singing, instrumental music, dancing, and drama that tells a story.* It was stylized and theatrical, and had effects for their own sakes—all characteristics of Baroque art.

The **oratorio,** *a piece for solo voices, chorus, and orchestra, was an expanded dramatic work on a literary or religious theme presented without theatrical action.* One of the most famous oratorios is George Frideric Handel's *Messiah,* composed in 1741. This piece contains the famous "Hallelujah Chorus."

Another vocal form was the **cantata,** *a collection of vocal compositions with instrumental accompaniment consisting of several movements based on related secular or sacred text segments.* Movements alternated among chorus, solo, duet, and/or trio.

Baroque music is often performed today by orchestras, choirs, and smaller instrumental and vocal ensembles, both in sacred and secular settings. You might explore your community for places where Baroque music is performed.

Check Your Understanding

Recall

1. Describe some major characteristics of the Baroque period, reflected in its music and art.

2. Describe instrumental music during the Baroque period by identifying both popular instruments and some instrumental forms that were composed.

3. Identify three vocal music forms of the Baroque period.

4. Describe an oratorio, and name a famous Baroque oratorio. Who composed it?

Thinking It Through

1. Compare Renaissance and Baroque music by explaining the similarities and differences between both styles.

2. What characteristics of the Baroque period explain why people of this period enjoyed opera? Why do people in today's society still enjoy Baroque operas?

Listening to . . .
Baroque Music

Handel — *Messiah*
"There were shepherds"

George Frideric Handel (1685–1759) was a musical prodigy. He was a favorite composer of the aristocracy in England where he wrote for all occasions. After Handel had written many operas he turned to writing oratorios, which brought him lasting recognition. An oratorio is a large-scale musical work for solo voices, chorus, and orchestra, that is performed without staging or costuming generally based on a Biblical story. One of Handel's most famous works is *Messiah*, which he wrote in 24 days.

Bach — *The Well-Tempered Clavier*
"Prelude and Fugue in C Minor"

Johann Sebastian Bach (1685–1750) was born in Eisenach, Germany. Born into a family of musicians, Bach played organ and clavichord and sung in churches by the age of 15. He was a devout man of the Lutheran faith, whose hymn tunes, known as chorales, figured prominently in much of his sacred music. During his time as church organist, Bach wrote more than 140 chorales for organ. The *Well-Tempered Clavier*, composed in 1722, contains a prelude and fugue in each of the twelve major and minor keys. These indicate the inexhaustible richness of Bach's artistry, for in each set, he produced entirely fresh versions of these types.

BAROQUE CONNECTIONS

Introducing . . .

"Sound the Trumpet"

Henry Purcell

Setting the Stage

This vivacious little duet is the fourth movement of the birthday ode, "Come Ye Sons of Art, Away" written in 1694 for the birthday of Queen Mary. Because of its text, it can be used for almost any festive occasion, including programs of Christmas music. The piano accompaniment has retained the "figured bass" or "basso continuo" that appeared in all choral and church music during the Renaissance and therefore, the practice carried over into many scores of the Baroque period. Feel the almost instrumental texture of this choral piece as you practice and perform it.

Meeting the Composer

Henry Purcell (1659–1695)

Born in London, Henry Purcell was one of the greatest English composers of the Baroque period. Unfortunately, his career was cut short after only 20 years. He wrote in almost every genre of his day. Purcell was the organist at Westminster Abbey and later for the Chapel Royal. He wrote superb organ music, motets, and service music, but his anthems may be his greatest contribution. Purcell was also asked to provide music for special occasions such as coronations or royal weddings. Purcell created a considerable amount of secular music in the areas of solo songs, chamber music, and operas. The anthem that you are about to learn, "Sound the Trumpet," is similar to many other anthems written by Purcell and is designed for small vocal groups with orchestral accompaniment.

Sound the Trumpet

COMPOSER: *Henry Purcell* (1659–1695)
EDITED BY: *James Erb*

CHORAL MUSIC TERMS
embellishment
part independence
sixteenth notes

VOICING
SA

PERFORMANCE STYLE
Not too fast, lilting
Accompanied by piano

FOCUS
- Read, clap, and sing rhythms with sixteenth notes.
- Read and sing parts with melodic embellishment.
- Sing one of two parts with independence.

Warming Up

 Rhythm Drill
Clap the following exercise as someone keeps the steady beat. Sometimes the parts are together, and sometimes they are independent. However, they always have the same steady beat. Read one measure at a time, and listen to the other part. Then put it all together.

Vocal Warm-Up

Sing the exercise using the syllables provided. The *h* sound at the beginning of each syllable will help propel the air toward the pure vowel sound. Repeat the exercise up or down a half step.

Continue up or down by half steps to work on pure vowels and beginning "h" sound.

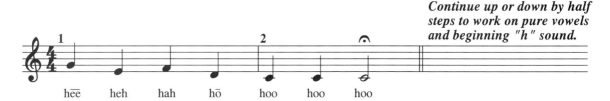

hēē   heh   hah   hō   hoo   hoo   hoo

Sight-Singing

Read and sing this exercise using solfège and hand signs or numbers. Use these parts for either voice part. Switch parts and sing again.

Singing: "Sound the Trumpet"

Oh, those trumpets!

You know the sound of trumpets. What feelings do trumpets bring to mind? What do you know about the history of trumpets? Read the text of "Sound the Trumpets," and write the phrases down without the repetition. What do the words mean?

Now turn to the music for "Sound the Trumpet" on page 144.

HOW DID YOU DO?

? ?

The trumpet sounds to celebrate success. Think about your preparation and perform-ance of "Sound the Trumpet."

1. How successfully can you clap rhythms with sixteenth notes? Clap the Rhythm Drill with a classmate to demonstrate.

2. Choose a phrase with melodic embellishment of text in "Sound the Trumpet" and perform it with a classmate.

3. Describe your ability to maintain part independence. Describe the choir's ability as a group.

4. How does "Sound the Trumpet" reflect the characteristics of the Baroque period?

Sound the Trumpet

(From the Birthday Ode, "Come, Ye Sons of Art," 1694)

Henry Purcell (1659–1695)
Edited by James Erb

SA with Piano Accompaniment

L.G. Co., 787

* Purcell's figuration stops here.

L.G. Co., 787

* pronounced: o'-boy

L.G. Co., 787

L.G. Co., 787

The Oath of the Horatii reflects Jacques Louis David's (1748–1825) interest in the beauty of Greco-Roman subjects. This interest in idealistic Classical subjects has a parallel in the formal structures of much of the music composed during this period.

1786. Jacques Louis David. *The Oath of the Horatii.* (Detail.) Oil on canvas. 3.35 x 4.27 m   (11' x 14). Toledo Museum of Art, Toledo, Ohio.

Classical Period

COMPOSERS

Franz Joseph Haydn (1732–1809)
Wolfgang Amadeus Mozart (1756–1791)
Ludwig van Beethoven (1770–1827)
Vincento Bellini (1801–1835)

ARTISTS

Francois Boucher (1703–1770)
Jean-Honoré Fragonard (1732–1806)
Francisco Gôya (1746–1828)
Jacques Louis David (1748–1825)

AUTHORS

Voltaire (1694–1778)
Wolfgang Goethe (1749–1832)
Jane Austen (1775–1817)

After completing this lesson, you should be able to:

- Compare qualities of music written in the Classical and Baroque styles.
- Identify two major composers from the Classical period.
- Define sonata form.

Today, we have a fascination with the old. We are excited to climb pyramids or see the ruins of ancient civilizations. We glorify stories that contain archeological subjects. The **Classical period** (1750–1820) was *a time when society began looking to the ancient Greeks and Romans for examples of order and ways of looking at life.*

The Classical Period—a Time of Balance, Clarity, and Simplicity

Baroque music was written with an emotional quality that was rather flamboyant. Embellishments and virtuosity dominated compositions. In comparison, music of the Classical period gave the expression of emotion a more restrained quality. Clarity, repose, and balance took an upper hand in expressing emotion in Classical music.

In the eighteenth century, painters, sculptors, and architects took notice of the ancient Greek and Roman artifacts being excavated in Athens, Pompeii, and other archeological sites. The calmness and simplicity of this ancient, "classical" art inspired logic, symmetry, and balance and guided artists away from the overly decorative, exaggerated ideals of the Baroque.

CHORAL MUSIC TERMS
Classical period
sonata-allegro form

▲ **The Classical period reflects the renewal of interest once again in the design elements of balance, symmetry, and simplicity of line. Commissioned by Napoleon, the Arc de Triomphe du Carrousel was inspired by the Arch of Septimus Severus in Rome.**

1806. Charles Percier and Pierre F. L. Fontaine. The Arc de Triomphe in the Place du Carrousel. Arc de Triomphe du Carrousel, Paris, France.

Swift writes
Gulliver's Travels

▼ 1726

George Washington

▼ 1732–1799

Thomas Jefferson

▼ 1743–1826

▲ 1732–1757
Franklin writes *Poor Richard's Almanac*

Music of the Classical Period

During the Classical period, people developed an interest in knowing more about the cultural aspects of life, such as art and music, that had once been attainable only by the wealthy. More books were published for learning about music. Musical scores were also more widely available. Musicians, mainly supported by the wealthy and aristocratic, now wrote music that was accessible to the general public.

The two main composers associated with this period are Franz Joseph Haydn (1732–1809) and Wolfgang Amadeus Mozart (1756–1791). The large quantity and variety of their work and their faithfulness to the Classical style overshadowed many other composers of the time. Ludwig van Beethoven was born in 1770 and began composing in this period, but his work bridges the gap between the Classical and Romantic periods, the latter of which will be discussed later.

The idea of improvisation and exaggerated use of embellishments of the Baroque were abandoned for a more precise and balanced style in the Classical period. A balance between content of the music and the form in which it was expressed became an essential characteristic of the period.

Symphonies, sonatas, concertos, and chamber works became important vehicles in instrumental works. During this time, the **sonata-allegro form,** *a movement written in* A B A *form*, was born. In this form, there is a section, the *Exposition*, which represents the theme (A). The theme is then repeated with elaboration (A'). Many times this elaboration was improvised by the performer on the spot, and was a sign of his or her musical skills. The next section of the piece, the *Development*, was a contrasting section (B). Finally, there was a return to the original theme (A) in a section called *Recapitulation*.

Opera experienced a great reformation in the eighteenth century. Composers felt a need to remove its excess vocal acrobatics and to emphasize its drama.

Classical Music Today

You can hear Classical music performed in many places today. A Mozart Festival is held every summer in many cities in the United States. Classical music is performed in concert halls by choirs, instrumental groups, and soloists the world over. You may even hear Classical music used in television or radio commercials. Advertisers use the music to create a certain mood.

American Revolutionary War fought
1775–1783

Federal Government established in America
1789

1775
James Watt invents the steam engine

1789
French Revolution begins

1808
Roman excavations begin at Pompeii, Italy

1776
American Declaration of Independence signed

Check Your Understanding

Recall

1. What is the main difference between the Baroque and Classical styles?

2. What are the main characteristics of Classical music?

3. Name two composers who wrote during the Classical period.

4. What form was very important in instrumental compositions of the Classical period? Describe the form.

5. How did opera change during the Classical period?

Thinking It Through

1. How did the Greek and Roman cultures influence the Classical period?

2. Was the music of the Classical period enjoyed by all people, or by just the wealthy? Explain your answer.

3. If you wanted to hear examples of Classical music today, where could you find them?

4. Are there any similarities between characteristics of the Classical period and those of the society you live in today?

Listening to . . .

Classical Music

CHORAL SELECTION

Mozart — The Marriage of Figaro: Act I, (Scene 6) "Non so piu"

"Non so piu" from The Marriage of Figaro is an aria performed by Cherubino, a young page, who is in love with love itself. The Marriage of Figaro (written in 1786), is a comic opera or "opera buffa" and revolves around the marriage of a valet, Figaro, and a maid, Susanna. The plot has many comical confusions, jealousies, and deceptions. The part of Cherubino is played by a soprano in a trouser role.

INSTRUMENTAL SELECTION

Beethoven — Piano Sonata in C Minor (Pathétique) "First Movement"

The "First Movement" in Ludwig van Beethoven's (1770–1827) Piano Sonata in C minor (Pathétique) is one of three "chapters" in the sonata. Each movement is designed to be complete in itself, yet not complete the story. Listen to the tragedy in the first movement that engulfs the listener and tells the tragic tale.

CLASSICAL CONNECTIONS

Introducing . . .
"Ave Verum Corpus"

Wolfgang Amadeus Mozart

Setting the Stage

Composed in 1791 when he was 35, Mozart's "Ave Verum Corpus" is a well-known choral piece. It has balanced harmony and fluid line, (for example, measures 22–37), free from exaggerations, giving this piece an elegant, refined quality found in music from the Classical period. Although "Ave Verum Corpus" was written for a four-part mixed choir, the clarity and simplicity within the music still equalizes the text with the music in this two-part arrangement. The beauty and emotion of the music is blended masterfully with the text.

Meeting the Composer
Wolfgang Amadeus Mozart (1756–1791)

Born in Salzburg, Austria, Wolfgang Amadeus Mozart, whose full name is Johann Chrysostom Wolfgang Theophilus, began his musical career at an extremely early age. By the time he was four years old, Mozart had already mastered the keyboard and by age five had written his first musical piece. He became a master of the violin quickly thereafter. Mozart's father, Leopald Mozart, recognized Amadeus' talent and began a tour through Europe, exhibiting his son's extraordinary talents. By age 16, Mozart had already written nearly 25 symphonies.

"Ave Verum Corpus" was written for Anton Stoll, a choirmaster and friend of Mozart's, for use as a funeral motet.

Ave Verum Corpus

COMPOSER: *Wolfgang Amadeus Mozart (1756–1791)*
ARRANGER: *John Leavitt*

CHORAL MUSIC TERMS
adagio
crescendo
decrescendo
Latin
phrasing
tuning

VOICING
Two part

PERFORMANCE STYLE
Adagio
Accompanied by keyboard

FOCUS
- Sing a sustained, connected phrase.
- Tune with another part while singing.
- Sing using correct Latin pronunciation.

Warming Up

Vocal Warm-Up 1

Sing on *loo*. Face a partner, standing with one foot in front of the other, hands clasped. As you sing the crescendo pull outward with even tension between you. Release the tension slowly during the decrescendo. Feel the pull of the phrase as you connect the notes to form a phrase.

Vocal Warm-Up 2

Sing the first four pitches detached on the syllable *hoh*. Sing the second four on one connected *hoh*. Think of all eight pitches as one phrase. Repeat moving up by half steps.

Sight-Singing

Read and sing this exercise using solfège and hand signs or numbers. Listen and carefully tune each pitch. Notice that the first and third pitches sound the same in the first two measures.

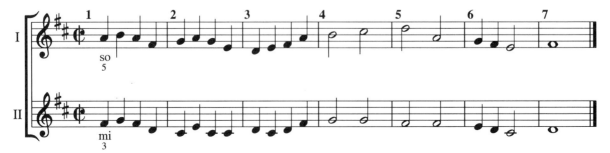

Singing: "Ave Verum Corpus"

Show a phrase with movement.

Place your hands on your lap, then raise both hands slowly above your head. Now raise your hands while counting slowly to eight, reaching all the way up on eight, then slowly lowering hands for eight counts. Try to make a very smooth movement for the 16-beat phrase.

Now turn to the music for "Ave Verum Corpus" on page 158.

HOW DID YOU DO?

? ?

You can describe your success in this lesson with phrases and sentences. Think about your preparation and performance of "Ave Verum Corpus."
1. Describe what you learned about singing phrases correctly, then demonstrate with a classmate by singing a phrase of "Ave Verum Corpus."

2. What does it mean to tune with another part while singing? What do you have to do?
3. Describe how you would know you performed well.
4. How does "Ave Verum Corpus" reflect the characteristics of the Classical period?

Ave Verum Corpus

Wolfgang Amadeus Mozart (1756–1791)
Arranged by John Leavitt

Two-part, Accompanied

*This is a keyboard realization of the original string parts.

SV9215

*The ornament is played on the beat.

SV9215

ta - tum in mor - tis ex - a - mi -

prae - gus - ta - tum in mor - tis ex - a - mi -

ne, in mor - tis ex -

ne, in mor - tis ex -

a - mi - ne.

a - mi - ne.

Emotional response is the significant feature in *Wounded Feelings* by English artist Alice Walker. Interest in exploring feelings and reactions, rather than formal structure, is typical of visual arts and music during the **Romantic period.**

1862. Alice Walker. *Wounded Feelings*. Oil on canvas. 101.6 x 76.2 cm (40 x 30"). The Forbes Magazine Collection, New York, New York.

Romantic Period

After completing this lesson, you should be able to:

- Compare qualities of music written in the Romantic and Classical styles.
- Identify two major composers from the Romantic period.
- Define nationalism, art songs, *and the* Romantic period.

Whenever there are rules, they are challenged by some people. The **Romantic period** (1820–1900) was *a time in which artists and composers attempted to make a break from classical music ideas.* The eighteenth century came to a close, leaving behind a restrained and controlled era, and the nineteenth century brought a newly acquired political and artistic freedom. There was a revolutionary spirit in society, with ideals of liberty and individualism, dramatic action, and indepentent thought. The musical restraints and order of the Classical period soon gave way to experimentation, as composers became impatient with the older rules and traditions.

The Romantic Period—a Time of Drama

Most composers of the Romantic period kept many of the classical forms alive. However, it is their treatment of these forms that made new statements about music. **Symphonies**—large orchestral pieces for many instruments, usually of three or four parts or movements—began to become popular. In some symphonies, a chorus was added (e.g., Beethoven's *Ninth Symphony*).

Many composers based their works on legends, dramas, or novels. In doing so, they explored through their music the heights and depths of human emotion. This innovation contrasted with previous vocal and instrumental works, many of which required musical simplicity. In general, vocal melodies became longer and more expressive, harmonies became more colorful, and instrumentation was expanded to enhance the overall possibilities of tone color in the music. Freedom and flexibility of rhythm and form brought new hues to the palette of sound composed by Romantic period composers.

Music of the Period

During the Romantic period, a new class of people—landowners, merchants, businesspeople who were not nobles—gained a powerful place in society. We refer to them as the middle class. With the help of the Industrial Revolution, which created many jobs, more and more people entered this class and took an active part in their culture and their nation. A growing pride in patriotism brought a spirit of nationalism to music. **Nationalism** in music

COMPOSERS

Ludwig van Beethoven (1770–1827)
Franz Schubert (1797–1828)
Hector Berlioz (1803–1869)
Felix Mendelssohn (1809–1847)
Frédéric Chopin (1810–1849)
Robert Schumann (1810–1856)
Franz Liszt (1811–1886)
Richard Wagner (1813–1883)
Giuseppe Verdi (1813–1901)
Clara Schumann (1819–1896)
Georges Bizet (1828–1875)
Modest Mussorgsky (1839–1881)
Johannes Brahms (1833–1897)
Peter Ilyich Tschaikovsky (1840–1893)
Giacomo Puccini (1858–1924)

ARTISTS

Élisabeth Vigée-Lebrun (1755–1842)
Rosa Bonheur (1822–1899)
Edouard Manet (1832–1883)
Edgar Degas (1834–1917)
Paul Cezanne (1839–1906)
Claude Monet (1840–1926)
Berthe Morisot (1841–1895)
Pierre Auguste Renoir (1841–1919)
Mary Cassatt (1845–1926)
Vincent van Gogh (1853–1890)
Georges Seurat (1859–1891)
Alice Walker ( )

AUTHORS

Noah Webster (1758–1843)
Mary Wollstonecraft Shelley (1797–1851)
Ralph Waldo Emerson (1803–1882)
Elizabeth Barrett Browning (1806–1861)
Henry Wadsworth Longfellow (1807–1882)
Edgar Allan Poe (1809–1849)
Harriet Beecher Stowe (1811–1896)
Theodore Dostoyevsky (1821–1881)
Leo Tolstoy (1828–1910)

CHORAL MUSIC TERMS

art songs
nationalism
Romantic period
symphonies

Louisiana Purchase
established
▼ **1803**

Abraham Lincoln
▼ **1809–1865**

Frederick Douglass
▼ **c. 1817–1895**

Mary Baker Eddy
▼ **1821–1910**

Monroe Doctrine created
▼ **1823**

▲ **1804**
Napoleon crowned Emperor

▲ **1812–1814**
U.S. declares war on Britain

▲ **1821**
Jean Champollion deciphers Egyptian
hieroglyphics using the Rosetta Stone

▲ **The glass-and-iron Crystal Palace was erected for the 1851 Great Exhibition in Hyde Park, London. Its naves and transepts housed the Handel Orchestra and Choir, concert halls, and exhibits of paintings and sculptures.**

1851. Vincent Brooks. Crystal Palace. Lithograph. Victoria and Albert Museum, London, Great Britain.

means that composers created works that evoked *pride in a country's historical and legendary past.* Richard Wagner wanted to preserve German music and legends in his operas. Giuseppe Verdi, great Italian composer of opera, felt he should guide the younger generation to adhere to the Italian historical and cultural tradition. This nationalism spawned interest in folk music of particular nations and regions. Robert Schumann used or imitated German folk songs. The American composer Stephen Foster composed songs on themes of life in the southern United States.

The art song became the most important vocal form during the Romantic period. **Art songs** were *expressive songs about life, love, and human relationships for solo voice and piano.* The most prolific composer of art songs, known in German as *lieder,* was Franz Schubert. Others were Robert Schumann and Johannes Brahms.

Modern Innovations

The idea of "selling" music to an audience through the musicians who composed it was developed during this time. In an effort to capture the general public's interest, a colorful and controversial personal life became an important factor in the visibility of many composers. Some of these composers were Franz Liszt, Hector Berlioz, and Richard Wagner.

Another figure to emerge in the performance setting was the music critic. His or her job was not only to explain the composer and the composer's music to the public, but also to set standards in musical taste.

Mary Mason Lyon founds Mt. Holyoke Female Seminary

1837

Jane Addams and Ellen Starr
found Hull House

1889

Motion picture camera patented by Thomas
Edison; sound recording developed

1898

1835–1910

Mark Twain

1844–1900

Friedrich Nietzsche

1895

Wireless telegraph developed by Marconi

The Romantic Period in Retrospect

The Romantic period was a time of exploration, imagination, and diversity. This period was diverse and complex, and it would be hard to describe with one definition all the new styles that emerged during it. The Romantic movement, however, was international in scope and influenced all the arts. The excitement of the Romantic period came from the rejection and challenge of old ways and a search for new, unique, and meaningful possibilities.

Check Your Understanding

Recall

1. Write one sentence which characterizes the mood of the Romantic period.

2. How did vocal melodies change during the Romantic period?

3. How did instrumental music change during the Romantic period?

4. Describe nationalism.

5. Define art song.

6. Name a Romantic composer of each: opera, art song.

Thinking It Through

1. Compare musical characteristics of the Classical and Romantic periods.

2. What was the role of the individual in music of the Romantic period?

3. Why was a music critic more likely to emerge during the Romantic period than before?

Listening to . . .

Romantic Music

CHORAL SELECTION

Bizet — *Carmen Act I, "Dans l'air"*

Carmen is considered to be the masterpiece of Georges Bizet (1828–1875), who began writing the opera in the winter 1872. This opera was different from contemporary in that the main action was not expressed through the dialogue, but rather through the music. When *Carmen* was put to stage, it was not readily accepted by the public and it wasn't until after Bizet's death in March 1875 that it became more popular.

INSTRUMENTAL SELECTION

Mendelssohn — *A Midsummer Night's Dream "Overture"*

Felix Mendelssohn was a child prodigy whose musical improvisation fascinated Germany's greatest poet, Goethe. A *Midsummer Night's Dream* was one of his most successful works and was written when he was 17. The march, often performed at weddings, is taken from his music to A *Midsummer Night's Dream* and was composed many years after the overture to this work.

ROMANTIC CONNECTIONS

Introducing . . .

"Abendlied"

Felix Mendelssohn

Setting the Stage

During the Romantic period some forms of music took on shorter forms. Composers such as Mendelssohn, Schubert, Chopin, and Brahms experimented with dances style pieces on the piano, vocal solos with piano accompaniment, called "lieder" and short programmatic orchestral or choral music. "Abendlied" reflects some of the styles of the Romantic period. It is similar to a folk song or lullaby supported by a beautiful piano accompaniment much like the lieder of the day. Brahms and Mendelssohn wrote many choral pieces for women's chorus and liked to set poems to music. Have fun with this. It paints a beautiful picture.

Meeting the Composer

Felix Mendelssohn (1809–1847)

Felix Mendelssohn was born in Hamburg, Germany in 1809. He was considered one of the foremost composers of the Romantic period. Born to a family of great wealth, Mendelssohn had every educational advantage to explore music with the finest teachers. He showed this musical talent at an early age by writing music by the age of 17. His early compositions included overtures and symphonies. He loved to travel especially in England and became one of the first composers of Queen Victoria. By age 24, he was conducting in Leipzig and in 1842, he established the Leipzig Conservatory. His later works included symphonies, programmatic overtures, concertos for different instruments, chamber music, and sonatas. Mendelssohn is also remembered for his discovery and revival of Bach's *St. Matthew Passion.* Much of Mendelssohn's choral music shows a strong influence from Bach.

Evening Song (Abendlied)

COMPOSER: *Felix Mendelssohn-Bartholdy* (1809–1847)
TEXT: *Heinrich Heine* (1797–1856)
TRANSLATOR: *Victor Prahl*

CHORAL MUSIC TERMS

abendlied

fermata

light upper range

phrasing

tranquillo

VOICING

SA

PERFORMANCE STYLE

Andante e tranquillo
Accompanied by piano

FOCUS

- Sing in the upper register with a light, flexible tone.
- Read and perform rhythms with accuracy.
- Sing using correct German pronunciation.

Warming Up

Vocal Warm-Up

Sing on the neutral syllable, then repeat moving up by half steps. As you get higher, the *o* sound will help lift the soft palate at the back of your mouth so you get a lighter sound.

Sight-Singing

Practice clapping the rhythm of each pattern first, then sing each pattern with solfège and hand signs or numbers. Don't go too fast just because there are sixteenth notes. Combine these patterns in different ways to see which combinations of two, three, and/or four parts you like.

Singing: "Evening Song (Abendlied)"

Can your ears see?

Listen to the text of "Evening Song," then draw or sketch an image that it brings to your mind. It doesn't have to be a picture of something—it might be just colors or shapes. Save this picture until after you learn "Evening Song."

Now turn to the music for "Evening Song" on page 170.

HOW DID YOU DO?

? ? ?

Your ears will let you know if you have learned new skills and ideas in this lesson. Think about your preparation and performance of "Evening Song."
1. What is your range? Can you sing in the upper register with a light, flowing sound?
2. Clap the rhythm of measures 5–18 of "Evening Song" to show how well you know the rhythms.
3. Choose a verse of "Evening Song (Abendlied)" to demonstrate your German pronunciation. How good is your German?

4. How does "Evening Song (Abendlied)" reflect the characteristics of the Romantic period?
5. Look at your drawing and listen to "Evening Song." Do you still feel the same about the text as you did when you first heard it? Why or why not?

Evening Song
Abendlied

Felix Mendelssohn-Bartholdy (1809–1847)
Original German text by Heinrich Heine (1797–1856)
English version by Victor Prahl

Soprano and Alto Voices

No. 392-03001

No. 392-03001

No. 392-03001

Three Musicians, a Cubist work by Pablo Picasso (1881–1973), demonstrates visual art based on geometric elements. In art and music, contemporary artists employ a variety of new techniques in the creation of their works.

1921. Pablo Picasso. *Three Musicians*. (Detail.) Oil on canvas. 200.7 x 222.9 cm (6'7" x 7'3¾"). Museum of Modern Art, New York, New York. Mrs. Simon Guggenheim Fund.

Contemporary Period

After completing this lesson, you should be able to:

- Compare qualities of music written in the Romantic and Contemporary styles.
- Identify several characteristics and styles of twentieth-century music.
- Define dissonance, twelve-tone music, and aleatoric, or chance music.
- Define fusion.

You live in the **Contemporary period,** *the time from* 1900 *to right now,* so you know something about contemporary music. More likely, however, there are some kinds of contemporary music that are still awaiting your discovery. One of the most important characteristics of the twentieth century has been rapid change. In this century, humans have lived through two world wars, the Chinese and Russian revolutions, the Great Depression, the Cold War, the rise and fall of Communism in many countries of the world, and many other events. Society is moving fast, and changes are constant.

A Time of Variety

Technology has had a large influence in the twentieth century, and it affects the preferences and demands of people. First, phonographs made music easily accessible to anyone who wanted to hear it. The invention of the radio brought live performances right into people's homes. Then, television captivated the world. Now tape recorder/players, CDs, and computers with interactive programs are popular, bringing us higher quality sounds and images and more possibilities. In many locations, synthesizers are taking the place of acoustic instruments, making it less expensive and easier for everyone to be involved in music-making and listening.

Looking Back

In the Romantic period, composers searched for new means of musical expression through the use of changed musical elements and larger orchestras. Many times, they were painting a story or mood in sound. As we have seen in the past, the artistic cycle tends to go from emotional to rational and back. During the twentieth century, composers and artists looked toward the abstract as a reaction to the overly emotional Romantic arts. They felt music was its own justification—it did not exist to paint some picture or evoke some emotion. Consequently, great changes occurred.

COMPOSERS

Richard Strauss (1864–1949)
Ralph Vaughan Williams (1872–1958)
Charles Ives (1874–1954)
Béla Bartók (1881–1945)
Igor Stravinsky (1882–1971)
Sergei Prokofiev (1891–1953)
Lorenz Hart (1895–1942)
George Gershwin (1898–1937)
Aaron Copland (1900–1990)
Richard Rodgers (1902–1979)
Benjamin Britten (1913–1976)
Leonard Bernstein (1918–1990)
Bob Dylan (1941–)

ARTISTS

Henri Rousseau (1844–1910)
Wassily Kandinsky (1866–1944)
Henri Matisse (1869–1954)
Pablo Picasso (1881–1973)
Georgia O'Keeffe (1887–1986)
Jackson Pollock (1912–1956)
Andrew Wyeth (1917–)
Andy Warhol (1930–1987)

AUTHORS

George Bernard Shaw (1856–1950)
Sir Arthur Conan Doyle (1859–1930)
Edith Wharton (1862–1937)
Gertrude Stein (1874–1946)
Robert Frost (1874–1963)
James Joyce (1882–1941)
Virginia Woolf (1882–1941)
T. S. Eliot (1888–1965)
William Faulkner (1897–1962)
Ernest Hemingway (1899–1961)
John Steinbeck (1902–1968)
Maya Angelou (1928–)

CHORAL MUSIC TERMS

abstract
aleatoric music
chance music
Contemporary period
dissonance
fusion
twelve-tone music

Wright Brothers' flight

1903

Model-T Ford introduced

1908

1905

First motion picture
theater opens

1914–1918

World War I

▲ **Just as contemporary music explores new avenues of expression, the Chapel of Notre Dame du Haut is a unique style of architecture. The massive walls and the rounded roof reflect abstract sculpture of contemporary artists. At the same time, the design is suggestive of the strength and solidity of a medieval fortress.**

1955. Le Corbusier. Frontal view of Chapelle de Notre Dame du Haut. Chapelle de Notre Dame du Haut, Ronchamp, France.

During the Romantic period, there was a change from church- and patron-sponsored composition to commissions and the sale of compositions. As the emerging middle class became the main consumer of music, the aristocracy played a less important role. Musicians' income was now provided by the sale of concert tickets and published music. In the twentieth century, serious music is supported by large and small performing groups in most cities and large towns. There is also support from nonprofit organizations, colleges, and universities.

As the twentieth century draws to a close, we can look back and see the changes from Impressionism (music that creates a musical picture with a

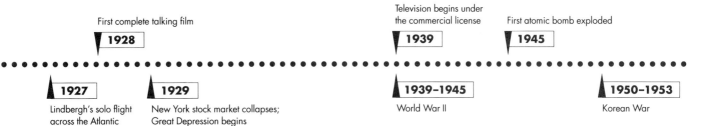

First complete talking film
1928

Television begins under
the commercial license
1939

First atomic bomb exploded
1945

1927
Lindbergh's solo flight
across the Atlantic

1929
New York stock market collapses;
Great Depression begins

1939–1945
World War II

1950–1953
Korean War

dreamy quality through chromaticism) to Expressionism (bold and dynamic expression of mood with great dissonance). Composers still use some forms from the Romantic period, such as opera, the symphony, and song form. Yet, they also continue to experiment with new ways to express themselves through music.

Music of the Period

Much of the music written before World War I was a continuation of Romanticism. After that war, composers were striving for a more objective style, a style stressing music for its own sake. There was a swing toward the **abstract,** *focusing on lines, rows, angles, clusters, textures, and form.*

Prior to the twentieth century, chords were built in intervals of a third. In the twentieth century, composers moved away from a tonal center and scalewise organization of pitch, and built *chords using seconds, fourths, fifths, and sevenths.* This resulted in a **dissonance** that sounded very harsh to those accustomed to tonal music.

Twelve-tone music was a new organization for composition. In twelve-tone music, *the twelve tones of the chromatic scale are arranged in a tone row, then the piece is composed by arranging and rearranging the "row" in different ways—backward, forward, in clusters of three or four pitches, and so on.* The mathematical possibilities are almost endless, especially when layered, instrument over instrument. Many people feel that music composed this way is more of an exercise for the composer than a source of pleasure for the listener.

Another interesting experimental type of music is **aleatoric,** or **chance music.** In aleatoric music, *the piece has a beginning and an end, and the rest is left to chance.* There is usually a score of some kind, but great freedom is allowed each performer (for example, how long to hold each pitch, which pitch to begin on, how fast to go, and when to stop).

Other compositional elements of the twentieth century include more angular contour of the melody and different concepts of harmony, which may emphasize dissonance, complex rhythms, and specific performance markings.

World Music and Fusion

During the twentieth century, folk music from around the world traveled to greater distances as people became more mobile. Immigrants and travelers shared songs from diverse cultures, and the musical styles have influenced one another. Popular music styles emerged and continue to be created, based on characteristics of different folk groups and the intermingling of ideas. Serious

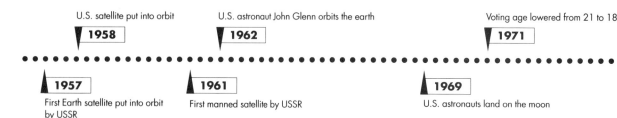

U.S. satellite put into orbit
1958

U.S. astronaut John Glenn orbits the earth
1962

Voting age lowered from 21 to 18
1971

1957
First Earth satellite put into orbit by USSR

1961
First manned satellite by USSR

1969
U.S. astronauts land on the moon

music composers also used the characteristics, melodies, and texts of folk music for their compositions. *Musical styles began to blend* in a phenomenon called **fusion.** For example, African-American, Cajun, and French Canadian musics have blended to create the fusion style called Zydeko. This kind of fusion is continuing today around the world.

There is also fusion of popular and art music styles. Many folk songs are being arranged and played by symphony orchestras. For example, vocalist Bobby McFerrin collaborated with classical cellist Yo-Yo Ma in recordings and performances with symphony orchestras. Popular singers such as Linda Ronstadt and Sting perform with professional choirs and orchestras. Instruments from many cultures find their way into classical performing groups, and music from all periods is being rearranged for electronic media.

Contemporary Pop Styles

Listed below are some American styles that have emerged during the twentieth century. Some of them are still thriving, and new ones are being created every day.

- *Ragtime*—an early style of jazz, very rhythmic and syncopated.
- *Musical Stage Music*—centered around Broadway and Hollywood musicals.
- *Blues*—simple, harmonious melodies with two phrases the same, then one different.
- *Spiritual*—songs originating in the slave culture, usually religious in theme.
- *Jazz*—strong but rhythmic understructure supporting solo and ensemble improvisation.
- *Rock*—strong, steady beat.
- *Country*—based on the folk style of the southern rural United States or on the music of the cowboy.
- *Folk*—folk songs and composed songs that tell a story or sometimes have a social message.
- *Reggae*—a fusion of rock and Jamaican rhythms, instruments, and language.
- *Calypso*—an island style with strong chords and syncopation.
- *Tejano*—a fusion of Mexican and country music.
- *Zydeko*—a fusion of African-American, Cajun, and French Canadian rhythms, instruments, and lyrics.

Music's Future and You

It is important that the consumer—that's you—has a sense of quality, in both popular and classical music. That way, quality music will survive into the future.

Little League accepts girls
▼ 1975

Fall of the Berlin Wall
▼ 1989

▲ 1972
Robert Moog patents the
Moog synthesizer

▲ 1975
U.S. withdraws from Vietnam

▲ 1976
U.S. celebrates its 200th birthday

Check Your Understanding

Recall

1. What technological inventions made music more accessible during the twentieth century?

2. Why did music change during the Contemporary period?

3. Are any forms from past periods still being composed? How are they different?

4. Describe dissonance.

5. Describe twelve-tone and aleatoric music.

6. Why is folk music still sung in the twentieth century? Name a folk song you have heard that is a twentieth-century piece.

7. Describe the result of fusion.

Thinking It Through

1. Some people say that records, tapes, and CDs are bad for society, because people never get together to sing or go out to concerts anymore. Do you think this is true? Why or why not? How do they affect the way we appreciate music?

2. If you wanted to see and hear examples of Contemporary art and popular music today, where could you find them?

Listening to . . .
Contemporary Music

CHORAL SELECTION

Rodgers — "My Funny Valentine"

Richard Rogers (1902–1979) was a self-taught American popular music and theatrical composer. In 1918, he and lyricist Lorenz Hart formed a team to create many bright and original scores for Broadway musicals. *Babes in Arms* (1937) was one of his highly praised musicals.

"My Funny Valentine" is from this musical. The song is a sentimental ballad sung by a traveler, Billie Smith. In this song, Billie Smith has just had her first lovers' quarrel. Lorenz Hart and Richard Rogers brought a new level of lyrics to musical comedies that were not based on clichés, but instead, on serious poetry.

INSTRUMENTAL SELECTION

Bartók — *Music for Strings, Percussion and Celesta*

Béla Bartók (1881–1945), a twentieth-century composer from Hungary, held a strong interest in his native folk and peasant music. His *Music for Strings, Percussion, and Celesta* is written for a double string orchestra with celesta, piano, harp, xylophone, timpani, and other percussion instruments. He stipulated that the two string orchestras be separated by the other instruments in the seating arrangement of the group. Bartók was known for his innovative use of form, and in this piece he varies the standard rondo form.

Introducing...

"Linden Lea"

Ralph Vaughan Williams

Setting the Stage

In "Linden Lea," Vaughan Williams tells a lovely Irish story, using long extended phrases and intricate rhythm patterns. This piece is beautifully written for women's voices. Have a good time practicing and performing "Linden Lea."

Meeting the Composer

Ralph Vaughan Williams (1872–1958)

Ralph Vaughan Williams, a twentieth-century English composer, had a versatile career as an organist, conductor, lecturer, teacher, editor, and writer. He greatly contributed to the development of twentieth-century music in Britain. For creative inspiration, he went to the roots of his home country, England, and combined the historic music of Tudor era, folk music, and his own musical ideas, to produce truly magnificent contemporary pieces of music.

He was the music editor of the English Hymnal. For this book he wrote the tune for the hymn "For All the Saints." His collection of folk songs contributed the three "Norfolk Rhapsodies" based on melodies from the region.

After serving in World War I, he continued to compose. Some of the cantatas that he wrote included "Dona Nobis Pacem" and "Hodie: Mass in G Minor" and "Te Deum in G Major for Double Chorus" and the motet "O Clap Your Hands." In addition, he composed many other symphonies, songs, ballets, and operas.

CONTEMPORARY LESSON

Linden Lea

COMPOSER: *Ralph Vaughan Williams* (1872–1958)

TEXT: W. *Barnes*

ARRANGER: *Douglas E. Wagner*

CHORAL MUSIC TERMS

andante con moto

breath mark

dynamics

no-breath mark

phrasing

VOICING

SSA

PERFORMANCE STYLE

Andante con moto

Accompanied by piano

FOCUS

- Read rhythms and pitches in three parts.
- Recognize and sing complete phrases.
- Recognize and sing correct dynamics.

Warming Up

Rhythm Drill

Clap the rhythm. Second sopranos should read the rhythms with the stems going down. Use crescendo and decrescendo to build and release tension in the phrase(s).

Vocal Warm-Up

Sing these chords using solfège and hand signs or numbers. Tune each chord.

Sight-Singing

Sight-sing this exercise using solfège and hand signs or numbers. Then, sing this exercise on *loo*. Notice the breath mark, and the no-breath mark. Work for a smooth, light sound throughout.

Singing: "Linden Lea"

How is a sentence like a phrase? Describe a complete sentence. Now describe a complete musical phrase. How are they related?

Just like it is important to speak and write in complete sentences, it is important to sing complete phrases.

Now turn to the music for "Linden Lea" on page 184.

HOW DID YOU DO?

?

Describe what you have learned. Think about your preparation and performance of "Linden Lea."
1. How well did you read in three parts? What was easy? What was difficult?
2. Discuss how to use breathing and dynamics to sing complete phrases.

Choose two classmates and a phrase to sing, demonstrating how to sing phrases.
3. How does "Linden Lea" reflect the characteristics of the Contemporary period? Does it have characteristics of any other period as well?

Linden Lea

Ralph Vaughan Williams (1872–1958)
Arranged by Douglas E. Wagner
Words by W. Barnes

Treble Voices, SSA, with Piano

HMC-944

Reprinted by permission.

Additional Performance Selections

VOICING

Two part

PERFORMANCE STYLE

Easily
Accompanied by keyboard

Alexander's Ragtime Band

Warming Up

Vocal Warm-Up

Sing this warm-up using solfège or numbers. Continue to move up and down stepwise.

Now turn to page **194.**

VOICING

Two part

PERFORMANCE STYLE

With spirit
Accompanied by piano

America, of Thee I Sing!

Warming Up

Vocal Warm-Up

Sing this Warm-Up using solfège and hand signs or numbers. Be sure your pitches are accurate. Try the same drill starting on high *do* and singing intervals downward.

Rhythm Drill

Find these three rhythm patterns in the music for "America, of Thee I Sing." Clap them by themselves, then clap the phrase they are found in.

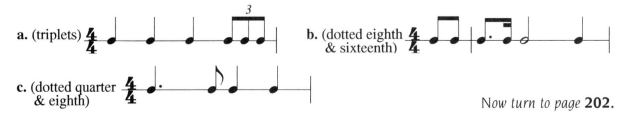

a. (triplets)

b. (dotted eighth & sixteenth)

c. (dotted quarter & eighth)

Now turn to page **202.**

VOICING

Two part

PERFORMANCE STYLE

Proudly
Accompanied by piano

Let Freedom Sing!

Warming Up

Vocal Warm-Up

Sing this exercise using solfège and hand signs or numbers. Sway right and left on alternating beats to feel the flowing of eighth notes and to give energy to your sound.

Continue up by half steps.

Now turn to page **208.**

VOICING

Three part

PERFORMANCE STYLE

With a light, 2-beat feel
Accompanied by piano

'Round the Riverside

Warming Up

Vocal Warm-Up

Sing this exercise using solfège and hand signs or numbers, then on *doo.* Add a clapping pattern, down to the right on beat 2, and up to the left on beat 4. Sing the vocal pattern.

Continue up by half steps.

Now turn to page **215.**

VOICING

Two-part chorus

PERFORMANCE STYLE

Accompanied by piano

Chumbara

Warming Up

Vocal Warm-Up

Sing using solfège and hand signs or numbers, then on *chum*. First sing it slowly, then try it with a quick lively bounce.

Continue up by half steps.
do do[1] ti la so fa mi re do
1 7 6 5 4 3 2 1
Chum chum chum etc...

Now turn to page **225.**

VOICING

Three-part treble

PERFORMANCE STYLE

Accompanied by hammer dulcimer

The Kalanta of the New Year

Warming Up

Vocal Warm-Up

Sing this exercise using solfège and hand signs or numbers. Sing it as a two-part canon, beginning after the third beat of the first full measure, where the star is. Think, listen, and hold your part in tune. Find these melodic segments in "The Kalanta of the New Year."

*

Now turn to page **231.**

VOICING

Three-part treble

PERFORMANCE STYLE

Freely
Accompanied by guitar
   or keyboard
Drum optional

Three Sephardic Folk Songs

Warming Up

Vocal Warm-Up

Read these two scales using solfège and hand signs or numbers. Notice that E is the tonal center for both scales. In the first, the E minor scale, E is *la*. In the second, the E Phyrgian scale, E is *mi*. Sing the scales several times to get the pitch relationships in your ears. Half the group will sing a drone on E as the other half improvises on the scale tones. This way, you will get used to this new sound.

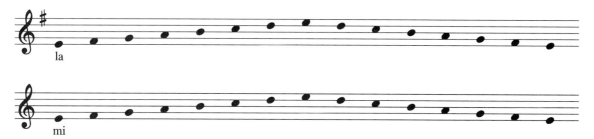

Now turn to page **236.**

Alexander's Ragtime Band

Words and Music by Irving Berlin
Additional material by Charlotte Lee
Arranged by Douglas E. Wagner (ASCAP)

Two-part Choir with Keyboard Accompaniment

Oh, my hon-ey, oh, my hon-ey, bet-ter hur-ry and let's me-an-der,

Ain't you go-in', ain't you go-in', to the lead-er man, rag-ged me-ter man?

hear, _____ come on and hear, _____ it's the best band in the land; _____ They can

Come on and hear, come on and hear, it's the best band in the land; _____

play a bu-gle call like you ne-ver heard be-fore,

So nat-u-ral that you'll al-ways ask for more;

It's just _____ the best band in the land, _____ hon-ey lamb. Come on a-

It's just _____ the best band in the land, _____ hon-ey lamb.

392-41693

392-41693

hear,____ come on and hear,____ it's the best band in the land;____ They can

Sax - es sway-in', ____ drums a - lay - in' down a syn-co-pat-ed beat.

play a bu - gle call like you nev - er heard be - fore, so nat - u - ral that you'll

al -ways ask for more; It's just____ the best band in the land,____

In rag-time rhy-thm, will all that's in 'em, they're mak - in' mu-sic

hon - ey   lamb. Come on a - long, _____ come on a - long, _____ let me

sweet and   fine. _   Clar - i -nets a-screech-in',   trum - pet - ers a-reach-in',

take   you   by   the   hand,   up to the man, _____ up to the

high   for notes out of   range,   And the crowd is danc - in',

man _____ who's the lead - er   of   the band, _____ and if you

sway - in', and ro-manc - in',   shuf - flin' off with each   new change; _____

392-41693

America, of Thee I Sing!

(A Partner Song with America, The Beautiful)

Mary Donnelly and George L. O. Strid
Arranged by George L. O. Strid

Two-part Voices and Piano

5808

which it stands, one na - tion un - der God, in - di -

vis - i - ble, with lib - er - ty and jus - tice for

all, with lib - er - ty and jus - tice

for _____ all.

*AMERICA, THE BEAUTIFUL, words by Katherine Lee Bates, music by Samuel A. Ward.

5808

shed His grace on thee, And crown thy good with broth - er - hood from sea to shin - ing sea.

5808

America, of Thee I Sing! **205**

Let Freedom Sing!

Mary Lynn Lightfoot

Two-part Chorus and Piano

Ranges:

H 5851-2

Reproduced with permission. Permit # 275772.

through hill and val - ley the mes-sage of lib - er - ty!_____ Let free-dom

through hill and val - ley the mes-sage of lib - er - ty!_____ Let free-dom

sing!

Free - dom's mel - o - dy

sing!

fills the sky with the col - ors of red, white, and blue.

H 5851-3

Free - dom's flag, ___ long may it wave, "O'er the land of the free ___

___ and home of the brave"!

Let free - dom sing, voic-es u - nit - ing, songs a - bout peace for all

Let free - dom sing, voic-es u - nit - ing, songs a - bout peace for all

* Quoting *"America the Beautiful,"* by Katherine L. Bates and Samuel A. Ward.
H 5851-5

H 5851-6

bove the fruit - ed plain!"

Let free-dom sing, voic-es u - nit - ing, songs a - bout peace for all

na - tions to hear! Let the bells ring, ech - o - ing loud - ly,

through hill and val-ley the mes-sage of lib-er-ty!____ Let free-dom

through hill and val-ley the mes-sage of lib-er-ty!____

62

sing! Let free-dom sing, "From sea to

Let free-dom sing,____ "From sea to

62

shin - ing sea"!

shin - ing sea"!

Dedicated to my sisters Marlene, Kay, Jackie and Pam

'Round the Riverside

Arranged by
Saundra Berry Musser (ASCAP)

Any Combination of Three-part Voices and Piano

7998

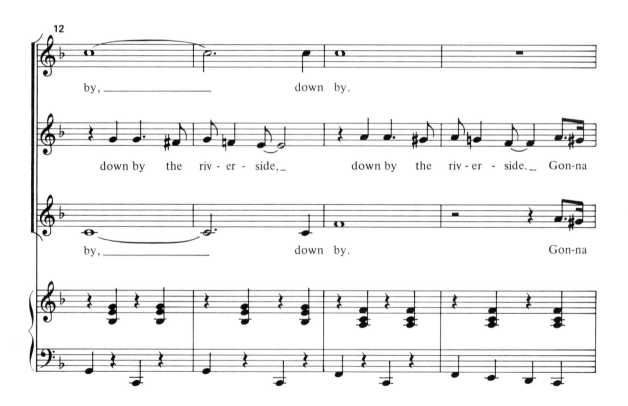

7998

Down by the riv - er. ___

Down by the riv - er. ___

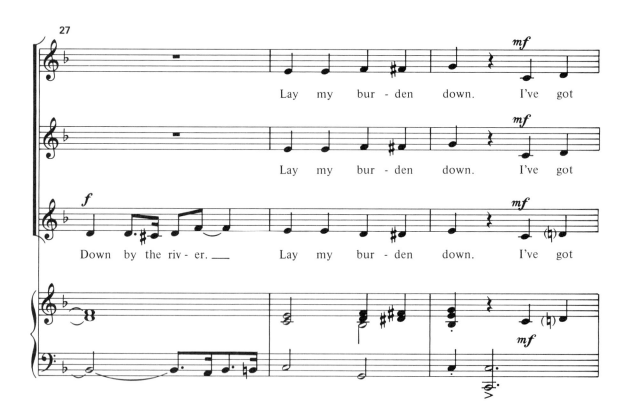

Lay my bur - den down. I've got

Lay my bur - den down. I've got

Down by the riv - er. ___ Lay my bur - den down. I've got

7998

7998

7998

Chumbara

French Canadian Folk Song
Arranged by Aden G. Lewis

Two-part Chorus and Piano

The Kalanta of the New Year (St. Basil's Day)

Traditional Greek Folk Song
English text and setting by
Malcolm Dalglish

Three-part Treble Voices with Hammer Dulcimer

dawn-ing of the year. All the child-ren in the street sing a bless-ing on Saint Ba - sil's

bless-ing on Saint Ba-sil's Day. It is the dawn-ing of the year. All the

child-ren in the street sing a bless-ing on Saint Ba - sil's Day. It is the

Day. It is the dawn-ing of the year. All the child-ren in the street in the

child-ren in the street sing a bless-ing on Saint Ba - sil's Day. It is the

dawn-ing of the year. All the child-ren in the street sing a bless-ing on Saint Ba - sil's

58

dawn - ing of_____ the year._____

dawn-ing of the year in our town. And all the child-ren in the street gath- er

Day. It is the dawn-ing of the year in our town. And all the

58

Three Sephardic Folk Songs

Arranged by
The Western Wind

I. IRME QUIERO

II. RAHELICA BAILA

Arranged by Lawrence Bennett
English text by William Zukof

Los ra- to- nes god- ros, E- llos dan las pal- mas.
Lit- tle mous- ies in a ring, Make them diz- zy clap- ping.
Am **Em** **B7** **Em**

(guitar tacet)
f
Ra- he- li- ca, Ra- he- li- ca, Ra- he- li- ca, Ra- he- li- ca,
f

Voices *p*
Ra- he- li- ca, Ra- he- li- ca, Ra- he- li- ca, Ra- he- li- ca,
mf
Ra- he- li- ca bai- la, Mo- xo- ni- co can- ta,
Lit- tle Ra- chel danc- ing, Lit- tle Mo- ses sing- ing,
Drum
p

Ra- he- li- ca, Ra- he- li- ca, Ra- he- li- ca, Ra- he- li- ca,
Los ra- to- nes god- ros, E- llos dan las pal- mas.
Lit- tle mous- ies in a ring, Make them diz- zy clap- ping.

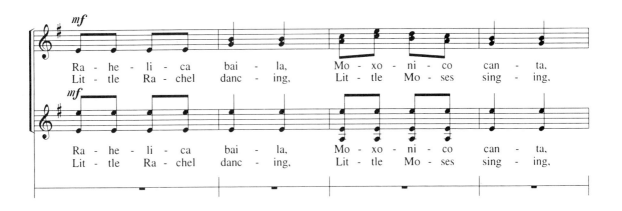

Ra - he - li - ca bai - la, Mo - xo - ni - co can - ta,
Lit - tle Ra - chel danc - ing, Lit - tle Mo - ses sing - ing,

Ra - he - li - ca bai - la, Mo - xo - ni - co can - ta,
Lit - tle Ra - chel danc - ing, Lit - tle Mo - ses sing - ing,

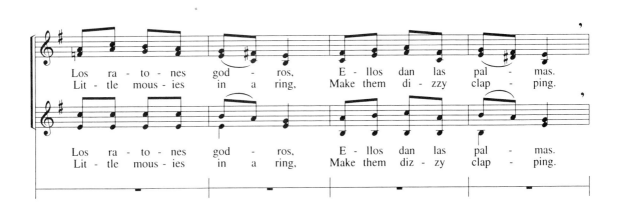

Los ra - to - nes god - ros, E - llos dan las pal - mas.
Lit - tle mous - ies in a ring, Make them diz - zy clap - ping.

Los ra - to - nes god - ros, E - llos dan las pal - mas.
Lit - tle mous - ies in a ring, Make them diz - zy clap - ping.

All Voices

Ra - he - li - ca bai - la, Mo - xo - ni - co can - ta,
Lit - tle Ra - chel danc - ing, Lit - tle Mo - ses sing - ing,

Guitar

Em   Em   Am   Em

Three Sephardic Folk Songs **239**

III. XINANÁY

3rd Verse English text by Elliot Z. Levine

Glossary

Choral Music Terms

A

a cappella   (ah-kah-PEH-lah) [It.] Unaccompanied vocal music.

accelerando   (*accel.*) (ah-chel-leh-RAHN-doh) [It.] Gradually increasing the tempo.

accent   Indicates the note is to be sung with extra force or stress. (ࣞ)

accidentals   Signs used to indicate the raising or lowering of a pitch. A sharp (♯) alters a pitch by raising it one-half step; a flat (♭) alters a pitch by lowering it one-half step; a natural (♮) cancels a sharp or a flat.

accompaniment   Musical material that supports another; for example, a piano or orchestra accompanying a choir or soloist.

adagio   (ah-DAH-jee-oh) [It.] Slow tempo, but not as slow as largo.

al fine   (ahl FEE-neh) [It.] To the end.

alla breve   Indicates cut time; duple meter in which there are two beats per measure, the half note getting one beat.

allargando   (*allarg.*) (ahl-ahr-GAHN-doh) [It.] To broaden, become slower.

aleatoric or chance music   Music in which chance is deliberately used as a compositional component.

allegro   (ah-LEH-groh) [It.] Brisk tempo; faster than moderato, slower than *vivace*.

allegro assai   (ah-LEH-groh ah-SAH-ee) [It.] Very fast; in seventeenth-century music, the term can also mean "sufficiently fast."

altered pitch   A note that does not belong to the scale of the work being performed.

alto   The lower female voice; sometimes called contralto or mezzo-soprano.

anacrusis   (a-nuh-KROO-suhs) [Gk.] *See* upbeat.

andante   (ahn-DAHN-teh) [It.] Moderately slow; a walking tempo.

andante con moto   (ahn-DAHN-teh kohn MOH-toh) [It.] A slightly faster tempo, "with motion."

animato   Quick, lively; "animated."

aria   (AHR-ee-uh) [It.] A song for a solo singer and orchestra, usually in an opera, oratorio, or cantata.

arpeggio   (ahr-PEH-jee-oh) [It.] A chord in which the pitches are sounded successively, usually from lowest to highest; in broken style.

art song   Expressive songs about life, love, and human relationships for solo voice and piano.

articulation   Clarity in performance of notes and diction.

a tempo

a tempo   (ah TEM-poh) [It.] Return to the established tempo after a change.

B

balance and symmetry   Even and equal.

baritone   The male voice between tenor and bass.

bar line   (measure bar) A vertical line drawn through the staff to show the end of a measure. Double bar lines show the end of a section or a piece of music.

Baroque period   (buh-ROHK) [Fr.] Historic period between c. 1600 and c. 1750 that reflected highly embellished styles in art, architecture, fashion, manners, and music. The period of elaboration.

bass   The lowest male voice, below tenor and baritone.

bass clef   Symbol at the beginning of the staff for lower voices and instruments, or the piano left hand; usually referring to pitches lower than middle C. The two dots lie on either side of the fourth-line F, thus the term, F clef.

beat   A steady pulse.

bel canto   (bell KAHN-toh) [It.] Italian vocal technique of the eighteenth century with emphasis on beauty of sound and brilliance of performance.

binary form   Defines a form having two sections (A and B), each of which may be repeated.

breath mark   A mark placed within a phrase or melody showing where the singer or musician should breathe. (؍)

C

cadence   Punctuation or termination of a musical phrase; a breathing break.

caesura   (si-ZHUR-uh) [Lt.] A break or pause between two musical phrases. (//)

call and response   A song style that follows a simple question-and-answer pattern in which a soloist leads and a group responds.

calypso style   Folk-style music from the Caribbean Islands with bright, syncopated rhythm.

cambiata   The young male voice that is still developing.

canon   A compositional form in which the subject is begun in one group and then is continually and exactly repeated by other groups. Unlike the round, the canon closes with all voices ending together on a common chord.

cantata   (kan-TAH-tuh) [It.] A collection of vocal compositions with instrumental accompaniment consisting of several movements based on related secular or sacred text segments.

cantabile   In a lyrical, singing style.

chantey   (SHAN-tee) [Fr.] A song sung by sailors in rhythm with their work.

chant, plainsong   Music from the liturgy of the early church, characterized by free rhythms, monophonic texture, and sung *a cappella*.

chorale   (kuh-RAL) [Gr.] Congregational song or hymn of the German Protestant (Evangelical) Church.

chord   Three or more pitches sounded simultaneously.

chord, block   Three or more pitches sounded simultaneously.

chord, broken   Three or more pitches sounded in succession; *see also* arpeggio.

chromatic   (kroh-MAT-ik) [Gr.] Moving up or down by half steps. Also the name of a scale composed entirely of half steps.

Classical period   The period in Western history beginning around 1750 and lasting until around 1820 that reflected a time when society began looking to the ancient Greeks and Romans for examples of order and ways of looking at life.

clef   The symbol at the beginning of the staff that identifies a set of pitches; *see also* bass clef and treble clef.

coda   Ending section; a concluding portion of a composition. (⊕)

common time   Another name for 4/4 meter; *see also* cut time. (𝐜)

composer   The creator of musical works.

compound meter   Meter whose beat can be subdivided into threes and/or sixes.

con   (kohn) [It.] With.

concerto   Composition for solo instrument and an orchestra, usually with three movements.

consonance   A musical interval or chord that sounds pleasing; opposite of dissonance.

Contemporary period   The time from 1900 to right now.

continuo   A Baroque tradition in which the bass line is played "continuously," by a cello, double bass, and/or bassoon while a keyboard instrument (harpsichord, organ) plays the bass line and indicated harmonies.

contrapuntal   *See* counterpoint.

counterpoint   The combination of simultaneous parts; *see* polyphony.

crescendo   (*cresc.*) (kreh-SHEN-doh) [It.] To gradually become louder.

cued notes   Smaller notes indicating either optional harmony or notes from another voice part.

cut time   2/2 time with the half note getting the beat. (¢)

D

da capo   (*D.C.*) (dah KAH-poh) [It.] Go back to the beginning and repeat; *see also* dal segno and al fine.

dal segno   (*D.S.*) (dahl SAYN-yoh) [It.] Go back to the sign and repeat. (𝄋)

D. C. al fine   (dah KAH-poh ahl FEE-neh) [It.] Repeat back to the beginning and end at the "fine."

decrescendo   (*decresc.*) (deh-kreh-SHEN-doh) [It.] To gradually become softer.

delicato   Delicate; to play or sing delicately.

descant   A high, ornamental voice part often lying above the melody.

diction   Clear and correct enunciation.

diminuendo   (*dim.*) (duh-min-yoo-WEN-doh) [It.] Gradually getting softer; *see also* decrescendo.

diphthong   A combination of two vowel sounds consisting of a primary vowel sound and a secondary vowel sound. The secondary vowel sound is (usually) at the very end of the diphthong; for example, in the word *toy*, the diphthong starts with the sound of "o," then moves on to "y," in this case pronounced "ee."

dissonance   Discord in music, suggesting a state of tension or "seeking"; chords using seconds, fourths, fifths, and sevenths; the opposite of consonance.

divisi   (*div.*) (dih-VEE-see) [It.] Divide; the parts divide.

dolce   (DOHL-chay) [It.] Sweet; *dolcissimo*, very sweet; *dolcemente*, sweetly.

Dorian mode   A scale with the pattern of whole-step, half, whole, whole, whole, half, and whole. For example, D to D on the keyboard.

dotted rhythm   A note written with a dot increases its value again by half.

double bar   Two vertical lines placed on the staff indicating the end of a section or a composition; used with two dots to enclose repeated sections.

doubling   The performance of the same note by two parts, either at the same pitch or an octave apart.

downbeat   The accented first beat in a measure.

D. S. al coda   (dahl SAYN-yoh ahl KOH-dah) [It.] Repeat from the symbol (𝄋) and skip to the coda when you see the sign. (⊕)

D. S. al fine   (dahl SAYN-yoh ahl FEE-neh) [It.] Repeat from the symbol (𝄋) and sing to fine or the end.

duple   Any time signature or group of beats that is a multiple of two.

duet   Composition for two performers.

dynamics   The volume of sound, the loudness or softness of a musical passage; intensity, power.

enharmonic   Identical tones that are named and written differently; for example, C sharp and D flat.

ensemble   A group of musicians or singers who perform together.

enunciation   Speaking and singing words with distinct vowels and consonants.

espressivo   (*espress.*) (es-preh-SEE-vo) [It.] For expression; *con espressione*, with feeling.

expressive singing   To sing with feeling.

exuberance   Joyously unrestrained and enthusiastic.

F _____

fermata   (fur-MAH-tah) [It.] A hold; to hold the note longer. (𝄐)

fine   (FEE-neh) Ending; to finish.

flat   Symbol (accidental) that lowers a pitch by one half step. (♭)

folk music   Uncomplicated music that speaks directly of everyday matters; the first popular music; usually passed down through the oral tradition.

form   The structure of a musical composition.

forte   (𝆑) (FOR-teh) [It.] Loud.

fortissimo   (𝆑𝆑) (for-TEE-suh-moh) [It.] Very loud.

freely   A direction that permits liberties with tempo, dynamics, and style.

fugue   (FYOOG) [It.] A polyphonic composition consisting of a series of successive melody imitations; *see also* imitative style.

fusion   A combination or blending of different genres of music.

G _____

grand staff   Two staves usually linked together by a long bar line and a bracket.

H _____

half step   The smallest distance (interval) between two notes on a keyboard; the chromatic scale is composed entirely of half steps, shown as (∨).

half time   *See* cut time.

harmonic interval   Intervals that are sung or played simultaneously; *see also* melodic interval.

harmony   Vertical blocks of different tones sounded simultaneously.

hemiola   (hee-mee-OH-lah) [Gk.] A metric flow of two against a metric flow of three.

homophonic   (hah-muh-FAH-nik) [Gk.] A texture where all parts sing similar rhythm in unison or harmony.

homophony   (hah-MAH-fuh-nee) [Gk.] Music that consists of two or more voice parts with similar or identical rhythms. From the Greek words meaning "same sounds," homophony could be described as "hymn-style."

hushed   A style marking indicating a soft, whispered tone.

I _____

imitation, imitative style   Restating identical or nearly identical musical material in two or more parts.

improvised   Invented on the spur of the moment.

improvisation   Spontaneous musical invention, commonly associated with jazz.

interval   The distance from one note to another; intervals are measured by the total steps and half steps between the two notes.

intonation   The degree to which pitch is accurately produced in tune.

introduction   An opening section at the beginning of a movement or work, preparatory to the main body of the form.

K _____

key   The way tonality is organized around a tonal center; *see also* key signature.

key change   Changing an initial key signature in the body of a composition.

key signature   Designation of sharps or flats at the beginning of a composition to indicate its basic scale and tonality.

L

legato   (leh-GAH-toh) [It.] Smooth, connected style.

ledger lines   Short lines that appear above, between treble and bass clefs, or below the bass clef, used to expand the notation.

leggiero   (leh-JEH-roh) [It.] Articulate lightly; sometimes nonlegato.

linear flow, line   Singing/playing notes in a flowing (smooth) manner, as if in a horizontal line.

lullaby   A cradle song; in Western music, usually sung with a gentle and regular rhythm.

M

madrigal   A secular vocal form in several parts, popular in the Renaissance.

maestoso   (mah-eh-STOH-soh) [It.] Perform majestically.

major (key, scale, mode)   Scale built on the formula of two whole steps, one half step, three whole steps, one half step.

Major 2nd   The name for an interval of one whole step or two half steps. For example, from C to D.

Major 6th   The name for an interval of four whole steps and one-half step. For example, from C to A.

Major 3rd   The name for an interval of two whole steps or four half steps. For example, from C to E.

major triad   Three tones that form a major third *do* to *mi* and a minor third *mi* to *so* as in C E G.

marcato   (mahr-KAH-toh) [It.] Long but separated pitches; translated as marked.

mass   The main religious service of the Roman Catholic Church. There are two divisions of mass: the Proper of the Mass in which the text changes for each day, and the Ordinary of the Mass in which the text remains the same for every mass. Music for the mass includes the Kyrie, Gloria, Credo, Sanctus, and Agnus Dei as well as other chants, hymns, and psalms. For special mass occasions composers through the centuries have created large musical works for choruses, soloists, instrumentalists, and orchestras.

measure   The space from one bar line to the next; also called bars.

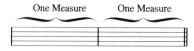

medieval   Historical period prior to the Renaissance, c. 500-1450.

medley   A group of tunes, linked together and sung consecutively.

melisma (n.) or melismatic (adj.)   (muh-LIZ-mah or muh-liz-MAT-ik) [Gk.] A term describing the setting of one syllable of text to several pitches.

melodic interval   Intervals that are performed in succession; *see also* harmonic interval.

melody   A logical succession of musical tones; also called tune.

meter   The pattern into which a steady succession of rhythmic pulses (beats) is organized.

meter signature   The divided number at the beginning of a clef; 4/4, 3/4, and so forth; *see also* time signature.

metronome marking   A sign that appears over the top line of the treble clef staff at the beginning of a piece indicating the tempo. It shows the kind of note that will get the beat and the numbers of beats per minute as measured by a metronome; for example, ♪ = 100.

mezzo forte   (*mf*) (MEHT-soh FOR-teh) [It.] Medium loud.

mezzo piano   (*mp*) (MEHT-soh pee-AH-noh) [It.] Medium soft.

middle C   The note that is located nearest the center of the piano keyboard; middle C can be written in either the treble or bass clef.

minor (key, scale) Scale built on the formula of one whole step, one half step, two whole steps, one half step, two whole steps.

Letter Names:	D	E	F	G	A	B♭	C	D
Movable Do:	la	ti	do	re	mi	fa	so	la
Numbers:	6	7	1	2	3	4	5	6

minor mode One of two modes upon which the basic scales of Western music are based, the other being major; using W for a whole step and H for a half step, a minor scale has the pattern W H W W H W W.

minor triad Three tones that form a minor third (bottom) and a major third (top), such as A C E.

minor third The name for an interval of three half steps. For example, from A to C.

mixed meter Frequently changing time signatures or meters.

moderato Moderate.

modulation Adjusting to a change of keys within a song.

molto Very or much; for example, *molto rit.* means "much slower."

monophonic (mah-nuh-FAH-nik) [Gk.] A musical texture having a single melodic line with no accompaniment; monophony.

monophony (muh-NAH-fuh-nee) [Gk.] One sound; music that has a single melody. Gregorian chants or plainsongs exhibit monophony.

motive A shortened expression, sometimes contained within a phrase.

musical variations Changes in rhythm, pitch, dynamics, style, and tempo to create new statements of the established theme.

mysterioso Perform in a mysterious or haunting way; to create a haunting mood.

N

nationalism Patriotism; pride of country. This feeling influenced many Romantic composers such as Wagner, Tchaikovsky, Dvořák, Chopin, and Brahms.

natural (♮) Cancels a previous sharp (♯) lowering the pitch a half step, or a previous flat (♭), raising the pitch a half step.

no breath mark A direction not to take a breath at a specific place in the composition. (♪ ⌐ ♪ or **N.B.**)

notation Written notes, symbols, and directions used to represent music within a composition.

O

octave An interval of twelve half steps; 8 or 8va = an octave above; 8vb = an octave below.

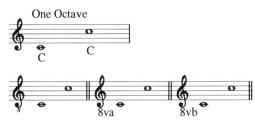

opera A combination of singing, instrumental music, dancing, and drama that tells a story.

optional divisi (*opt. div.*) Indicating a split in the music into optional harmony, shown by the smaller cued note.

oratorio A piece for solo voices, chorus, and orchestra, that is an expanded dramatic work on a literary or religious theme presented without theatrical action.

ostinato (ahs-tuh-NAH-toh) [It.] A rhythmic or melodic passage that is repeated continuously.

P

palate The roof of the mouth; the hard palate is forward, the soft palate (velum) is at the back.

parallel major and minor keys Major and minor keys having the same tonic, such as A major and A minor (A major being the parallel major of A minor and A minor the parallel minor of A major).

peak The high point in the course of a development; for example, the high point of a musical phrase or the high point in a movement of instrumental music.

pentatonic scale A five-tone scale constructed of *do, re, mi, so, la* (degrees 1, 2, 3, 5, 6) of a corresponding major scale.

Perfect 5th The name for an interval of three whole steps and one half step. For example, C to G.

Perfect 4th The name for an interval of two whole steps and one half step. For example, C to F.

phrase A musical sentence containing a beginning, middle, and end.

phrase mark In music, an indicator of the length of a phrase in a melody; this mark may also mean that the singer or musician should not take a breath for the duration of the phrase. (⌒)

phrasing The realization of the phrase structure of a work; largely a function of a performer's articulation and breathing.

pianissimo (*pp*) (pee-uh-NEE-suh-moh) |It.| Very soft.

piano (*p*) (pee-ANN-noh) |It.| Soft.

Picardy third An interval of a major third used in the final, tonic chord of a piece written in a minor key.

pick-up *See* upbeat.

pitch Sound, the result of vibration; the highness or lowness of a tone, determined by the number of vibrations per second.

piu (pew) |It.| More; for example, *piu forte* means "more loudly."

poco (POH-koh) |It.| Little; for example, *poco dim.* means "a little softer."

poco a poco (POH-koh ah POH-koh) |It.| Little by little; for example, *poco a poco cresc.* means "little by little increase in volume."

polyphony (n.) or polyphonic (adj.) (pah-LIH-fuh-nee or pah-lee-FAH-nik) |Gk.| The term that means that each voice part begins at a different place, is independent and important, and that sections often repeat in contrasting dynamic levels. Poly = many, phony = sounds.

presto (PREH-stoh) |It.| Very fast.

program music A descriptive style of music composed to relate or illustrate a specific incident, situation, or drama; the form of the piece is often dictated or influenced by the nonmusical program. This style commonly occurs in music composed during the Romantic period. For example, "The Moldau" from *Má Vlast*, by Bedřich Smetana.

progression A succession of two or more pitches or chords; also melodic or harmonic progression.

R

rallentando (*rall.*) (rahl-en-TAHN-doh) |It.| Meaning to "perform more and more slowly." *See also* ritardando.

recitative (res-uh-TAY-teev) |It.| A speechlike style of singing used in opera, oratorio, and cantata.

register, vocal A term used for different parts of a singer's range, such as head register (high notes) and chest register (low notes).

relative major and minor keys The relative minor of any major key or scale, while sharing its key signature and pitches, takes for its tonic the sixth scale degree of that major key or scale. For example, in D major the sixth scale degree is B (or *la* in solfège), *la* then becomes the tonic for A minor.

D major   B minor

Renaissance period The historic period in Western Europe from c. 1430 to 1600; the term means

"rebirth" or "renewal"; it indicates a period of rapid development in exploration, science, art, and music.

repeat sign A direction to repeat the section of music (‖:⫶‖); if the first half of this sign is omitted, it means to "go back to the beginning" (:‖).

repetition The restatement of a musical idea; repeated pitches; repeated "A" section in ABA form.

resolution (*res.*) A progression from a dissonant tone or harmony to a consonant harmony; a sense of completion.

resonance Reinforcement and intensification of sound by vibrations.

rest Symbols used to indicated silence.

rhythm The pattern of sounds and silences.

rhythmic motif A rhythmic pattern that is repeated throughout a movement or composition.

ritardando (*rit.*) The gradual slowing of tempo; also called "ritard."

Rococo Music of the Baroque period so elaborate it was named after a certain type of fancy rock work.

Romantic period A historic period starting c. 1820 and ending c. 1900 in which artists and composers attempted to break with classical music ideas.

rondo form An instrumental form based on an alternation between a repeated (or recurring) section and contrasting episodes (ABACADA).

root The bottom note of a triad in its original position; the note on which the chord is built.

round A composition in which the perpetual theme (sometimes with harmonic parts) begins in one group and is strictly imitated in other groups in an overlapping fashion. Usually the last voice to enter becomes the final voice to complete the song.

rubato (roo-BAH-toh) |It.| Freely; allows the conductor or the performer to vary the tempo.

S

sacred music Of or dealing with religious music; hymns, chorales, early masses; *see* secular music.

scale A pattern of pitches arranged by whole steps and half steps.

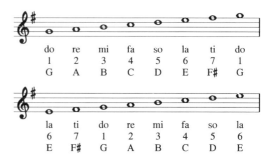

	do	re	mi	fa	so	la	ti	do
	1	2	3	4	5	6	7	1
	G	A	B	C	D	E	F♯	G

	la	ti	do	re	mi	fa	so	la
	6	7	1	2	3	4	5	6
	E	F♯	G	A	B	C	D	E

score The arrangement of instrumental and vocal staffs that all sound at the same time.

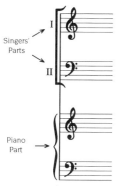

Singers' Parts

I

II

Piano Part

secular music Music without religious content; *see* sacred music.

sempre (SEHM-preh) [It.] Always, continually.

sequence Repetition of a pattern of notes on a higher or lower pitch level.

sequence

sharp A symbol (accidental) that raises a pitch by one half step. (♯)

sight-sing Reading and singing of music at first sight.

simile (*sim.*) (SIM-ee-leh) [It.] To continue in the same way.

simple meter Meter in which each beat is divisible by 2.

skip Melodic movement in intervals larger than a whole step.

slur Curved line placed over or under a group of notes to indicate that they are to be performed without a break. (◠)

solfège (SOHL-fehj) [Fr.] A method of sight-singing, using the syllables *do, re, mi, fa, so, la, ti,* etc. for pitches of the scale.

solo Composition for one featured performer.

sonata-allegro form (suh-NAH-tuh ah-LEH-groh) [It.] Large A B A form consisting of three sections: exposition, development, and recapitulation.

soprano The higher female voice.

sotto voce In a quiet, subdued manner; "under" the voice.

spirito (SPEE-ree-toh) [It.] Spirited; for example, *con spirito,* with spirit.

spiritual A type of song created by African Americans who combined African rhythms with melodies they created and heard in America.

staccato (stah-KAH-toh) [It.] Performed in a short, detached manner, as opposed to legato.

staff Series of five horizontal lines and four spaces on which music is written to show pitch.

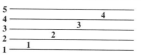

staggered entrances Voice parts or instruments begin singing or playing at different points within the composition.

steady beat A metrical pulse; *see also* beat, meter, rhythm.

step Melodic movement from one note to the next adjacent note, either higher or lower.

stepwise melodic movement Motion from one note to an adjacent one.

stress Emphasis on certain notes or rhythmic elements.

strong beat Naturally accented beats; beats 1 and 3 in 4/4 meter, beat 1 in 3/4 meter.

strophic Description of a song in which all the stanzas of the text are sung to the same music; opposite of *through-composed.*

style The particular character of a musical work; often indicated by words at the beginning of a composition, telling the performer the general manner in which the piece is to be performed.

subito (sub.) (SOO-bee-toh) [It.] Suddenly; for example, *sub. piano* means "suddenly soft."

suspension or suspended tone The tone or tones in a chord that are held as the remainder of the notes change to a new chord. The sustained tones often form a *dissonance* with the new chord, into which they then resolve.

sustained tone A tone sustained in duration; sometimes implying a slowing of tempo; *sostenuto* or *sostenendo,* abbreviated *sost.*

swing This is a performance style in which a pair of eighth notes (♪♪) are no longer performed evenly, but instead like a triplet (♪♪), yet they are still written (⌐3⌐ ♩♪); usually indicated at the beginning of a song or a section.

symphony An extended work in several movements, for orchestra; also an orchestra configured to perform symphonic music.

syncopation Deliberate shifts of accent so that a rhythm goes against the steady beat; sometimes referred to as the "offbeat."

T _____

tempo   A pace with which music moves, based on the speed of the underlying beat.

tempo I or tempo primo   Return to the first tempo.

tenor   A high male voice, lower than the alto, but higher than bass.

tenuto   (teh-NOO-toh) [It.] Stress and extend the marked note. ($\bar{\rho}$)

text   Words, usually set in a poetic style, that express a central thought, idea, moral, or narrative.

texture   The thickness of the different layers of horizontal and vertical sounds.

theme and variation form   A musical form in which variations of the basic theme comprise the composition.

tie   A curved line connecting two successive notes of the same pitch, indicating that the second note is not to be articulated. ($\rho\frown\rho$)

timbre   Tone color; the unique quality produced by a voice or instrument.

time signature   The sign placed at the beginning and within a composition to indicate the meter; for example, 4/4, 3/4; *see also* cut time, meter signature.

to coda   Skip to the ⊕ or CODA.

tonality   The organized relationships of pitches with reference to a definite key center. In Western music, most tonalities are organized by the major and minor scales.

tone   A sound quality of a definite pitch.

tone color, quality, or timbre   That which distinguishes the voice or tone of one singer or instrument from another; for example, a soprano from an alto or a flute from a clarinet.

tonic chord   (TAH-nik kord) [Gk.] The name of a chord built on the tonal center of a scale; for example, C E G or *do, mi, so* for C major.

tonic or tonal center   The most important pitch in a scale; *do*; the home tone; the tonal center or root of a key or scale.

tonic triad   A three-note chord comprising root, third, and fifth; for example, C E G.

treble clef   The symbol that appears at the beginning of the staff used for higher voices, instruments, or the piano right hand; generally referring to pitches above middle C, it wraps around the line for G, therefore it is also called the G-clef.

triad   A three-note chord built in thirds above a root tone.

trill   A rapid change between the marked note and the one above it within the same key. (*tr*⌁)

triplet   A group of notes in which three notes of equal duration are sung in the time normally given to two notes of equal duration.

troubadour   A wandering minstrel of noble birth in southern France, Spain, and Italy during the eleventh to thirteenth centuries.

tuning   The process of adjusting the tones of voices or instruments so they will sound the proper pitches.

tutti   (TOO-tee) [It.] Meaning "all" or "together."

twelve-tone music   Twentieth-century system of writing music in which the twelve tones of the chromatic scale are arranged into a tone row (numbered 1 to 12), and then the piece is composed by arranging and rearranging the "row" in different ways; for example, backward, forward, or in clusters of three or four pitches.

𝒰 _____

unison   Voice parts or instruments sounding the same pitches in the same rhythm simultaneously.

upbeat   A weak beat preceding the downbeat.

𝒱 _____

variation   *See* theme and variation form, musical variations.

vivace   (vee-VAH-chay) [It.] Very fast; lively.

voice crossing (or voice exchange)   When one voice "crosses" above or below another voice part.

𝒲 _____

whole step   The combination of two successive half steps. (⌐_⌐)

whole tone scale   A scale consisting only of whole steps.